suss design essentials

SUSS
DESIGN
ESSENTIALS

THE ULTIMATE COLLECTION FOR
A CLASSIC HANDKNIT WARDROBE

SUSS
DESIGN
ESSENTIALS

THE ULTIMATE COLLECTION FOR
A CLASSIC HANDKNIT WARDROBE

SUSS COUSINS

PHOTOGRAPHY BY SUZUKI K

A LARK PRODUCTION

POTTER
CRAFT

NEW YORK

Published in the United States by Potter Craft, an imprint of the Crown
Publishing Group, a division of Random House, Inc., New York.
www.crownpublishing.com
www.pottercraft.com

POTTER CRAFT and colophon, and POTTER and colophon are registered
trademarks of Random House, Inc.

Library of Congress Cataloging-in-Publication Data
Cousins, Suss.
Suss design essentials : the ultimate collection for a classic handknit wardrobe / photography
by Suzuki K. -- 1st ed.   p. cm.
Includes index.

  ISBN 978-0-307-34641-4

1. Knitting. 2. Knitting--Patterns. I. Title.
   TT820.C8558 2007

   746.43'2041--dc22

   2007004320

Printed in China

Design by Design MW / Doris Pesendorfer

10 9 8 7 6 5 4 3 2 1

First Edition

To all my employees, both past and present, at Suss Design, Inc.

SUSS DESIGN ESSENTIALS contents

introduction

This book is all about you—the modern woman. You are the woman that I think of each time that I sit down to sketch a new line of knitwear, the woman who wants to open her closet, grab something cool to wear, and feel attractive and comfortable the rest of the day and night. I imagine how busy and stressed today's women often are, and how wearing a beautiful sweater or dress can help us feel a little happier and a little more luxurious. I try to create knitwear that is timeless and classic but not too complicated, so it can become your wardrobe staple. My signature sweaters, coats, and dresses always involve a twist of some sort, such as special buttons, frayed or stitched edges, or asymmetrical closures. And unique yarns are a must for all my garments.

In fact, I begin all my designs with the yarn. I look at the yarn, handle it, and envision which stitch might bring out its best. Then I make swatches. I try knitting loosely and tightly and experiment with dropping stitches. When I am in love with my yarn and my swatch, I start to sketch. I have to knit smartly to make the most of each design's potential, combining the ideal stitch, yarn, and silhouette. And I have to think about the big picture, too, because I need to come up with a new line of 75–125 separates pieces four times a year.

Out of the hundreds of designs that I've produced in the last ten years, I have chosen my top thirty to appear in *Suss Design Essentials*. These designs are the most popular, the most wearable, the most flattering, and the most versatile—simply the best! Then I divided them into categories for easy reference: sweaters, separates, dresses, coats and capes, and those all-important accessories. You can "shop" for patterns in the book's chapters the same way you shop in the departments of a large store.

Many of these designs can be worn for all occasions. For me, there is no such thing as a division between a work day, an evening event, or the weekend. My life blurs together, and I need my wardrobe to be flexible. I might wear a T-shirt or blouse under a V-neck sweater at the studio and wear the same sweater alone for a sexier look when I go out to dinner. The pieces in this book can be combined in a million ways. Dressed up or dressed down with shoes and accessories, they'll take you from meetings to the movies.

Here you'll find a wider variety of yarns—from light to heavy—than in any of my previous books. Superchunky yarn is ideal for sweaters, while dresses call for a lighter yarn. Likewise, to keep things interesting as you knit, I've given you a rich variety of techniques and stitches including Fair Isle, cables, moss stitch, and double seed stitch. A few patterns are easy, but many are on the challenging side. The majority of the patterns call for increases and decreases and a substantial amount of finishing, which makes this a book for those who have knit a sweater or two.

I dreamed of being a fashion designer ever since I was a young girl watching my mother sew her own clothes. By the time I was nineteen, I had my own clothing boutique in my native Sweden. The boutique was called Thanks and it was a great education in what sold and what didn't. In time, I learned to buy the right things for my customers, which is not always easy!

When I started designing knitwear, I discovered that it's even harder to figure out which designs will be successful. A constant challenge in fashion is sizing. People come in different shapes and sizes, so I generally shy away from fitted designs. If I'm making a pattern, I use a fit model, plus mannequins in basic sizes that I developed sixteen years ago. Sometimes with knitwear, instead of creating a whole outfit, I concentrate on only one part—a sweater, for instance. So to keep the bigger picture in mind, I put together a large display with all the colors and shapes that I'm going to use for a particular line. Then I keep mixing and matching things until I'm happy with how it all looks together.

My inspiration comes from Scandinavia—a love of clean colors, lots of texture, and a need to keep warm during long winters. I look hard at everything around me from rocks, flowers, sky, and grass to city buildings, museums, art galleries, and jewelry. Of course, I also research what's happening on runways in Europe to keep up with all the high-fashion designers and their new lines.

After all the work that goes into creating a line, the big payoff for me is the day of the runway show. When the models come out one after the other wearing capes and coats and dresses and tops that I designed and I see the audience smiling because they can imagine wearing these clothes, I am 100 percent satisfied.

I hope that as you browse through *Suss Design Essentials,* you'll find many projects that will make you smile and think: I can't wait to knit that!

deep v-neck cable vest

I CAN STILL PICTURE MY GRANDFATHER WEARING HIS BROWN SWEATER-VEST TO KEEP WARM DURING THOSE LONG SWEDISH WINTERS. THIS IS A LONGER VERSION IN A CHUNKY CABLE KNIT. BECAUSE THE YARN IS A COTTON, THE VEST CAN BE WORN FOR THREE SEASONS. TRY PAIRING IT WITH A CRISP WHITE SHIRT FOR THE OFFICE. IF YOU SKIP THE SHIRT, THE V-NECK MAKES IT QUITE SEXY WHEN WORN WITH DENIM AND HIGH HEELS.

SIZES
SMALL (MEDIUM, LARGE)

FINISHED MEASUREMENTS
CHEST: 36" (38", 40")/91.5 (96.5, 101.5) CM
LENGTH: 35" (36", 37")/89 (91.5, 94) CM

YARN
10 (10, 11) SKEINS SUSS COTTON (100% COTTON;
2½ OUNCES/71 GRAMS; 118 YARDS/108 METERS),
COLOR CHOCOLATE

NOTIONS
1 PAIR SIZE 8 (5 MM) CIRCULAR NEEDLES, 24"/
61 CM (OR SIZE NEEDED TO OBTAIN GAUGE)
1 PAIR SIZE 9 (5.5 MM) NEEDLES (OR SIZE NEEDED
TO OBTAIN GAUGE)
1 CABLE NEEDLE

1 STITCH HOLDER
KNITTING ROW COUNTER (RECOMMENDED)
1 LARGE TAPESTRY NEEDLE
1 SIZE G (4 MM) CROCHET HOOK
SEWING PINS (OPTIONAL)

GAUGE
22 STITCHES AND 20 ROWS = 4"/10 CM IN TWO-BY-TWO RIB
STITCH WITH SIZE 8 NEEDLES
18 STITCHES AND 20 ROWS = 4"/10 CM IN CABLE PATTERN
WITH SIZE 9 NEEDLES
A NOTE ABOUT GAUGE: SINCE JUDGING CABLE GAUGE
CAN BE TRICKY, PLEASE DO A LARGE GAUGE SWATCH
AND MEASURE WHEN THE PIECE IS STRETCHED FLAT.

CABLE-10 PATTERN

Rows 1 and 3: Purl 2, knit 6, purl 2.

Rows 2 and 4: Knit 2, purl 6, knit 2.

Row 5: Purl 2, slip the next 3 stitches onto a cable needle and hold in back of work, knit the next 3 stitches from the left-hand needle, knit 3 stitches from the cable needle, purl 2.

Rows 6, 8, and 10: Knit 2, purl 6, knit 2.

Rows 7 and 9: Purl 2, knit 6, purl 2.

BACK

With smaller needles, cast on 80 (84, 88) stitches. Work in two-by-two rib stitch (knit 2, purl 2 until the end of the row) for 9 rows (2"/5 cm). Switch to the larger needles. Increase 1 stitch at the beginning and end of the next (wrong-side) row—82 (86, 90) stitches total. Work in the following cable pattern until the piece measures 28" (29", 29½")/71 (73.5, 75) cm from the cast-on edge, ending with a wrong-side row:

Row 1 (right-side rows): Knit 0 (0, 3), purl 2 (4, 2), knit 3 (3, 3), purl 2 (2, 2), [knit 3, work cable-10 pattern] 5 (5, 5) times, knit 3 (3, 3), purl 2 (2, 2), knit 3 (3, 3), purl 2 (4, 2), knit 0 (0, 3).

Row 2 (wrong-side rows): Purl 0 (0, 3), knit 2 (4, 2), purl 3 (3, 3), knit 2 (2, 2), [purl 3, work cable-10 pattern] 5 (5, 5) times, purl 3 (3, 3), knit 2 (2, 2), purl 3 (3, 3), knit 2 (4, 2), purl 0 (0, 3).

Repeat Rows 1 and 2. Maintain cable-10 pattern when shaping armhole and shoulder.

ARMHOLE SHAPING

Bind off 4 stitches at the beginning of the next two rows—74 (78, 82) stitches. Decrease 1 stitch at the beginning and end of every 2 rows 6 times—62 (66, 70) stitches. Work even until the piece measures 34" (35", 36")/86.5 (89, 91.5) cm from the cast-on edge.

SHOULDER SHAPING

Bind off 5 (5, 6) stitches at the beginning of the next 2 (6, 2) rows—52 (36, 58) stitches. Bind off 4 (0, 5) stitches at the beginning of the next 4 (0, 4) rows—36 (36, 38) stitches. Bind off loosely.

FRONT

Work as for the Back until armhole shaping. Bind off 4 stitches at the beginning of the next 2 rows—74 (78, 82) stitches. Next right-side row: Work 39 (41, 43) stitches and place the remaining 35 (37, 39) stitches on a stitch holder.

LEFT FRONT

Work from the needle. Bind off 4 stitches at the beginning of the next row. On armhole and shoulder edge, work shaping as described for the Back. *At the same time,* work even on the neckline edge for the next 2 rows. Decrease 1 stitch at the neckline edge every 2 rows (the beginning of every wrong-side row) 16 times.

RIGHT FRONT

Transfer stitches from the stitch holder to the needles. Work as for the Left Front but reverse shaping.

FINISHING

Weave in any loose ends with the tapestry needle.

Place the Front and Back pieces together with the right sides facing and pin them together. With the tapestry needle and yarn, sew the shoulder seams together using backstitch. Sew the side seams.

With the smaller needles, start at the bottom of the "V" neckline and pick up 116 (116, 124) stitches along the entire neckline. Work in two-by-two rib stitch for 1½"/3.8 cm, or approximately 8 rows. Bind off loosely in rib pattern.

Fold over the ends of the ribbed collar at the bottom center of the "V" neckline towards the wrong side of the piece. Fold the corners at a 45-degree angle to form a vertical line where the two edges meet at the bottom of the "V." With the tapestry needle and yarn, whipstitch this seam together securely. With the tapestry needle and yarn, tack down the edges of the collar on the wrong side of the sweater along the line of picked-up stitches.

With the crochet hook and yarn, start at the bottom of the armhole and work in single crochet stitch around the entire left armhole. Repeat for the right armhole.

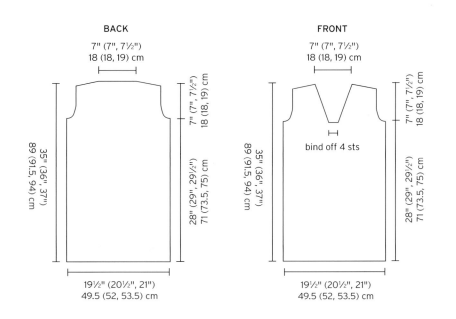

BACK
7" (7", 7½")
18 (18, 19) cm
7" (7", 7½")
18 (18, 19) cm
35" (36", 37")
89 (91.5, 94) cm
28" (29", 29½")
71 (73.5, 75) cm
19½" (20½", 21")
49.5 (52, 53.5) cm

FRONT
7" (7", 7½")
18 (18, 19) cm
7" (7", 7½")
18 (18, 19) cm
bind off 4 sts
35" (36", 37")
89 (91.5, 94) cm
28" (29", 29½")
71 (73.5, 75) cm
19½" (20½", 21")
49.5 (52, 53.5) cm

boyfriend sweater

THIS SWEATER'S OVERSIZED, LONG BODY, DROPPED SLEEVES, AND GRAY COLOR MIGHT MAKE IT LOOK CLASSIC AND CONSERVATIVE—BUT I ADDED A FASHION TWIST WITH THE VERY SEXY DEEP V-NECK AND THE UNRAVELED THREADS AROUND THE RIBBED EDGES. THINK OF THIS PIECE AS SOMETHING INSPIRED BY YOUR BOYFRIEND'S SWEATER—ALL COMFY AND WELL-WORN. WEAR IT OVER JEANS OR LEGGINGS FOR LOUNGING AROUND ON THE WEEKEND.

2

SIZES
SMALL (MEDIUM, LARGE)

FINISHED MEASUREMENTS
CHEST: 38" (40", 42")/96.5 (101.5, 106.5) CM
LENGTH: 28" (29", 30")/ 71 (73.5, 76) CM

YARN
9 (10, 11) SKEINS SUSS OLD FASHIONED (50% MERINO
    WOOL/40% COTTON/8% WOOL/2% POLYNUB;
    1.5 OUNCES/43 GRAMS; 126 YARDS/115 METERS),
    COLOR GRAY

NOTIONS
1 PAIR SIZE 9 (5.5 MM) NEEDLES
1 LARGE STITCH HOLDER
1 LARGE TAPESTRY NEEDLE
SEWING PINS (OPTIONAL)
SEWING NEEDLE AND OFF-WHITE THREAD

GAUGE:
18 STITCHES AND 20 ROWS = 4"/10 CM IN
    STOCKINETTE STITCH
22 STITCHES AND 20 ROWS = 4"/10 CM IN TWO-BY-TWO
    RIB STITCH

TWO-BY-TWO RIB STITCH PATTERN

Row 1: *Knit 2 stitches, purl 2 stitches*, repeat from * to * until 2 stitches remain, knit 2 stitches.

Row 2: Knit all knit stitches and purl all purl stitches.

Repeat Row 2.

BACK

Cast on 86 (90, 94) stitches. Work in two-by-two rib stitch pattern for 16 rows, or approximately 3"/7.5 cm.

Switch to stockinette stitch (knit all right-side rows and purl all wrong-side rows) and work even until the piece measures 20½" (21", 21½")/52 (53.5, 54.5) cm from the cast-on edge, or approximately 110 (112, 114) rows, ending with a wrong-side row.

ARMHOLE SHAPING

Cast on 7 stitches at the beginning of the next 2 rows—100 (104, 108) stitches total. To cast on stitches at the beginning of a row, insert the right-hand needle into the space between the first 2 stitches on the left-hand needle. Pull the yarn through, making a loop, and place that loop back on the left-hand needle. Repeat until you have added the necessary number of stitches.

Work even until the piece measures 26½" (27½", 28½")/67.5 (70, 72.5) cm, or approximately 134 (140, 144) rows, ending with a wrong-side row.

SHOULDER SHAPING

Bind off 8 (9, 10) stitches at the beginning of the next 6 (8, 4) rows. Bind off 10 (0, 9) stitches at the beginning of the next 2 (0, 4) rows. Bind off remaining 32 (32, 32) stitches.

FRONT

Work as for the Back until the piece measures 15½" (16½", 17½")/39.5 (42, 44.5) cm from the cast-on edge, or approximately 78 (82, 88) rows, ending with a wrong-side row.

To shape neckline, work 41 (43, 45) stitches. Knit 2 stitches together. Place the remaining 43 (45, 47) stitches on a stitch holder. Work from the needle for the left front. On the neckline edge, decrease 1 stitch every 4 rows 15 times. Along armhole and shoulder edges, work shaping as for the Back.

For right Front, pick up the remaining 43 (45, 47) stitches from stitch holder. Knit 2 stitches together along the neckline edge. Work as for the left Front but reverse shaping.

SLEEVES
(Make two)

Cast on 40 (40, 44) stitches. Work in two-by-two rib stitch for 16 rows, or approximately 3"/7.5 cm.

Switch to stockinette stitch. Increase 1 stitch at the beginning and end of every 9 (8, 8) rows 8 (10, 10) times—56 (60, 64) stitches total. Work even until the pieces measures 19" (20", 20½")/48 (51, 52) cm from the cast-on edge.

Bind off.

FINISHING

Weave in all loose ends with the tapestry needle.

With the tapestry needle and yarn, sew together the shoulder seams and side seams, using backstitch. Sew together the Sleeves using backstitch. Sew the Sleeves into the armholes. You may find it helpful to pin the pieces together first.

Using the photograph as a guide, whipstitch scraps of yarn around the edges of the sweater so that it appears you have mended holes.

COLLAR

Starting at the bottom center of the "V" neckline, pick up 68 stitches along the right neckline, 32 stitches along the back of the neck, and 68 stitches along the left neckline—168 stitches total. Work in a two-by-two rib stitch for 8 rows, approximately 1½"/3.8 cm.

Bind off in rib pattern.

Fold over the ends of the ribbed collar at the bottom center of the "V" neckline toward the wrong side of the piece. Fold the corners at a 45-degree angle to form a vertical line where the two edges meet at the bottom of the "V." With the sewing needle and thread, whipstitch this seam together securely. With the sewing needle and thread, tack down the edges of the collar on the wrong side of the sweater along the line of picked-up stitches.

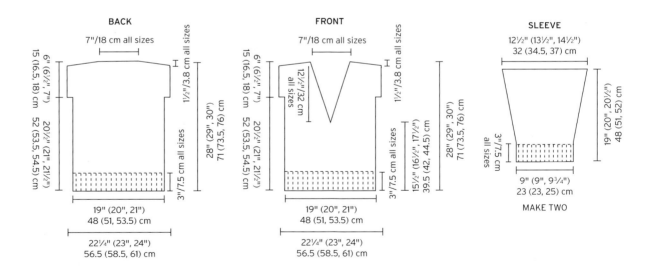

BACK

7"/18 cm all sizes

1½"/3.8 cm all sizes

6" (6½", 7") 15 (16.5, 18) cm

20½" (21", 21½") 52 (53.5, 54.5) cm

28" (29", 30") 71 (73.5, 76) cm

3"/7.5 cm all sizes

19" (20", 21") 48 (51, 53.5) cm

22¼" (23", 24") 56.5 (58.5, 61) cm

FRONT

7"/18 cm all sizes

1½"/3.8 cm all sizes

6" (6½", 7") 15 (16.5, 18) cm

12½"/32 cm all sizes

20½" (21", 21½") 52 (53.5, 54.5) cm

28" (29", 30") 71 (73.5, 76) cm

15½" (16½", 17½") 39.5 (42, 44.5) cm

3"/7.5 cm all sizes

19" (20", 21") 48 (51, 53.5) cm

22¼" (23", 24") 56.5 (58.5, 61) cm

SLEEVE

12½" (13½", 14½") 32 (34.5, 37) cm

19" (20", 20½") 48 (51, 52) cm

3"/7.5 cm all sizes

9" (9", 9¾") 23 (23, 25) cm

MAKE TWO

big-collar scandinavian sweater

THE FAIR ISLE USED IN THIS PROJECT IS A TRADITIONAL WAY OF KNITTING IN SCANDINAVIA. THIS SWEATER IS PERFECT FOR COZYING UP ON YOUR COUCH WHEN IT'S CHILLY OUTSIDE. I DESIGNED A SIMILAR VERSION FOR QUEEN LATIFAH TO WEAR IN HER MOVIE *LAST HOLIDAY*.

SIZES
SMALL (MEDIUM, LARGE)

FINISHED MEASUREMENTS
CHEST: 36" (39", 42")/91.5 (99, 106.5) CM
LENGTH: 31" (32", 33")/79 (81, 84) CM
(NOT INCLUDING COLLAR)

YARNS
A: 14 (15, 16) SKEINS SUSS ROYAL (45% NYLON/35%
VISCOSE/15% ACRYLIC/5% ALPACA; 2 OUNCES/57
GRAMS; 102 YARDS/93 METERS), COLOR JADE
B: 1 SKEIN SUSS SNUGGLE (60% COTTON/40% ACRYLIC;
2 OUNCES/57 GRAMS; 126 YARDS/115 METERS),
COLOR HONEY
C: 1 SKEIN SUSS SNUGGLE (60% COTTON/40% ACRYLIC;
2 OUNCES/57 GRAMS; 126 YARDS/115 METERS),
COLOR NATURALE

NOTIONS
1 PAIR SIZE 10 (6 MM) NEEDLES
1 PAIR SIZE 9 (5.5 MM) NEEDLES
2 YARN BOBBINS (RECOMMENDED FOR
FAIR ISLE TECHNIQUE)
SEWING PINS (RECOMMENDED)
1 LARGE TAPESTRY NEEDLE

GAUGE
16 STITCHES AND 20 ROWS = 4"/10 CM IN STOCKINETTE
STITCH WITH LARGER NEEDLES
16 STITCHES AND 20 ROWS = 4"/10 CM IN THREE-BY-THREE
RIB STITCH WITH LARGER NEEDLES
17 STITCHES AND 21 ROWS = 4"/10 CM IN THREE-BY-THREE
RIB STITCH WITH SMALLER NEEDLES

BACK

Cast on 72 (78, 84) stitches with yarn A and larger needles. Work in three-by-three rib stitch (knit 3, purl 3, repeat until the end of the row) pattern until the piece measures 3½"/9 cm, ending with a wrong-side row.

Switch to stockinette stitch (knit all right-side rows and purl all wrong-side rows). Work even for 4 rows.

Work 0 (2, 0) stitches and begin the 26-row Fair Isle pattern (you may find it helpful to work from yarn bobbins for yarn B and yarn C). For sizes Small and Large, switch to yarn indicated on the chart and begin the Fair Isle pattern where indicated on the chart. Repeat the stitch sequence in pattern until no stitches remain. For size Medium, switch to yarn indicated on the chart and begin the Fair Isle pattern where indicated on the chart. Repeat the stitch sequence until 2 stitches remain, and work the remaining stitches in yarn A.

With yarn A only, work even until piece measures 24½" (25", 26")/62 (63.5, 66) cm.

ARMHOLE SHAPING

Cast on 8 stitches at the beginning of the next 2 rows—88 (94, 100) stitches total. Work even until the piece measures 5½" (6", 6")/14 (15, 15) cm from the armhole shaping.

SHOULDER SHAPING

Bind off 12 (13, 15) stitches at the beginning of the next 2 (4, 2) rows—64 (42, 70) stitches. Bind off 11 (0, 14) stitches at the beginning of the next 2 (0, 2) rows—42 stitches remain.

COLLAR

Switch to smaller needles. Work the remainder of the stitches in three-by-three rib stitch. Increase 1 stitch at the beginning and end of every other row 15 times—72 stitches total. Work even until the collar measures 15"/38 cm from the end of the shoulder shaping.

Bind off loosely in rib pattern.

FRONT

Work the Front as for the Back.

SLEEVES (Make two)

Cast on 48 (54, 54) stitches with yarn A and larger needles. Work in three-by-three rib stitch until the piece measures 3½"/9 cm, ending with a wrong-side row.

Switch to stockinette stitch and work even for 4 rows.

Work 0 (2, 2) stitches and begin the 26-row Fair Isle pattern (you may find it helpful to work from yarn bobbins for yarn B and yarn C). For size Small, switch to yarn indicated on the chart and begin the Fair Isle pattern where indicated on the chart. Repeat the stitch sequence in pattern until no stitches remain. For sizes Medium and Large, switch to yarn indicated on the chart and begin the Fair Isle pattern where indicated on the chart. Repeat the stitch sequence until 2 stitches remain, and work the remaining stitches in yarn A.

With yarn A only, work even until the sleeve measures 11" (12", 12½")/28 (30.5, 32) cm, ending with a wrong-side row. Decrease 1 stitch at the beginning and end of the next (right-side) row—46 (52, 52) stitches. Decrease 1 stitch at the beginning and end of every 20 (12, 12) rows 1 (2, 2) time(s)—44 (48, 48) stitches total. Work even until the sleeve measures 18" (19", 19½")/46 (48, 49.5) cm.

Bind off.

FINISHING

Weave in all loose ends with the tapestry needle.

Place the Front and Back pieces together with the right sides facing. With the tapestry needle and yarn A, start at the sleeve edge and backstitch the shoulder and collar seams together. You may find it helpful to pin all the seams together first. To hide the seam when you wear the collar turned over, the first half of the collar should be worked with the right sides facing each other. Then turn the garment inside out and resume seaming the collar with the right sides facing out.

With the tapestry needle and yarn A, sew together the side seams using backstitch.

With the tapestry needle and yarn A, sew together the sleeve seams using backstitch.

With the tapestry needle and yarn A, sew the Sleeves into the armholes using backstitch. You may find it helpful to turn the piece inside out to do this.

FAIR ISLE CHART

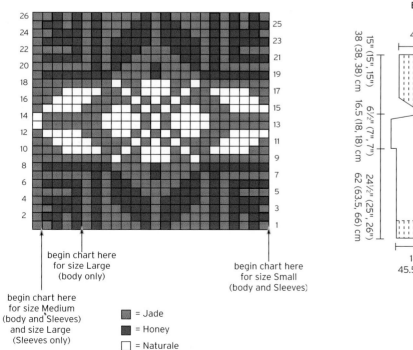

begin chart here
for size Large
(body only)

begin chart here
for size Small
(body and Sleeves)

begin chart here
for size Medium
(body and Sleeves)
and size Large
(Sleeves only)

■ = Jade
■ = Honey
□ = Naturale

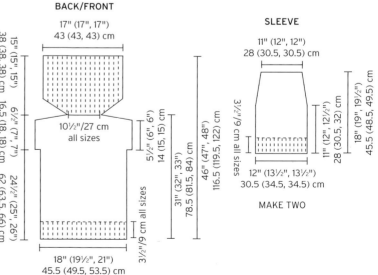

BACK/FRONT

17" (17", 17")
43 (43, 43) cm

15" (15", 15")
38 (38, 38) cm

6½" (7", 7")
16.5 (18, 18) cm

24½" (25", 26")
62 (63.5, 66) cm

10½"/27 cm
all sizes

5½" (6", 6")
14 (15, 15) cm

31" (32", 33")
78.5 (81.5, 84) cm

46" (47", 48")
116.5 (119.5, 122) cm

3½"/9 cm all sizes

18" (19½", 21")
45.5 (49.5, 53.5) cm

SLEEVE

11" (12", 12")
28 (30.5, 30.5) cm

3½"/9 cm all sizes

11" (12", 12½")
28 (30.5, 32) cm

18" (19", 19½")
45.5 (48, 49.5) cm

12" (13½", 13½")
30.5 (34.5, 34.5) cm

MAKE TWO

weekend boatneck pullover

GROWING UP IN SWEDEN, I OFTEN WENT SAILING WITH MY FRIENDS. ON THESE OUTINGS, I WORE REAL SAILOR PANTS IN LINEN WITH BUTTONS ON THE FRONT FLAP AND A SWEATER LIKE THIS ONE. KNIT IN NAVY AND WHITE STRIPES IN THE SOFTEST BABY ANGORA, THE SWEATER HAS CROCHET TIES AROUND THE BOTTOM AND ON THE BELL-SHAPED SLEEVES. IT'S GREAT FOR WEARING AT A RESORT OR ON A CRUISE OR FOR JUST HANGING AT HOME.

SIZES
SMALL (MEDIUM, LARGE, EXTRA-LARGE)

FINISHED MEASUREMENTS
CHEST: 34" (36", 38", 40")/86.5 (91.5, 96.5, 101.5) CM
LENGTH: 27" (28", 29", 30")/68.5 (71, 73.5, 76) CM

YARNS
A: 2 (2, 3, 4) SKEINS SUSS ANGORA (70% ANGORA/30%
NYLON; 1.5 OUNCES/43 GRAMS; 246 YARDS/225
METERS), COLOR NAVY
B: 2 (2, 3, 4) SKEINS SUSS ANGORA (70% ANGORA/30%
NYLON; 1.5 OUNCES/43 GRAMS; 246 YARDS/225
METERS), COLOR IVORY

NOTIONS
1 PAIR SIZE 4 (3.5 MM) NEEDLES (OR SIZE TO OBTAIN
GAUGE)
2 LARGE STITCH HOLDERS
2 SMALL STITCH HOLDERS
1 LARGE TAPESTRY NEEDLE
SEWING PINS
SEWING NEEDLE AND THREAD IN COMPLEMENTARY COLOR
1 SIZE G (4 MM) CROCHET HOOK

GAUGE
28 STITCHES AND 34 ROWS = 4"/10 CM IN
STOCKINETTE STITCH

STRIPE PATTERN FOR BACK AND FRONT

Rows 1–14: Work in yarn A.

Rows 15–28: Work in yarn B.

Repeat Rows 1–28.

STRIPE PATTERN FOR SLEEVES

Work 6 (4, 2, 0) rows in yarn B—6 (4, 2, 0) rows total.

Work 14 (14, 14, 10) rows in yarn A—20 (18, 16, 10) rows total.

Work (14 rows in yarn B and 14 rows in yarn A) 5 (5, 5, 6) times—160 (158, 156, 178) rows total.

Work 10 (14, 14, 0) rows in yarn B—170 (172, 170, 178) rows total.

Work 0 (6, 8, 0) rows in yarn A—170 (178, 178, 178) rows total.

BACK

Cast on 126 (132, 140, 146) stitches with yarn A. Work in stockinette stitch (knit all right-side rows and purl all wrong-side rows) and maintain the stripe pattern for the Back and the Front throughout.

Switch to yarn B and work even for 14 rows. Maintain the stripe pattern for the Back and the Front throughout.

Decrease 1 stitch at the beginning and end of every 28 (28, 28, 28) rows 5 (5, 5, 5) times—116 (122, 130, 136) stitches. Work even until the piece measures 21" (22", 22½", 23")/53.5 (56, 57, 58.5) cm, ending with a wrong-side row.

ARMHOLE SHAPING

Bind off 5 (7, 7, 7) stitches at the beginning of the next 2 rows—106 (108, 116, 122) stitches. Decrease 1 stitch at the beginning and end of every 2 (2, 2, 2) rows 25 (26, 28, 31) times—56 (56, 60, 60) stitches. Work 1 row even. Place the remaining 56 (56, 60, 60) stitches on a large stitch holder.

FRONT

Work the Front as for the Back.

SLEEVES (Make two)

For the three smaller sizes, cast on 78 (84, 90) stitches with yarn B. For the largest size, cast on 96 stitches with yarn A. Work in stockinette stitch following the stripe pattern for Sleeves.

Work even in the stripe pattern for Sleeves until the piece has 170 (178, 178, 178) rows, approximately 20" (21", 21", 21")/51 (53.5, 53.5, 53.5) cm.

ARMHOLE SHAPING

Bind off 5 (7, 7, 7) stitches at the beginning of the next 2 rows—68 (70, 76, 82) stitches. Decrease 1 stitch at the beginning and end of every 2 (2, 2, 2) rows 25 (26, 28, 31) times—18 (18, 20, 20) stitches. Work 1 row even. Place the remaining 18 (18, 20, 20) stitches on a small stitch holder.

FINISHING

Weave in all loose ends with the tapestry needle.

Place the Front and the Back pieces together with the right sides facing each other. Pin the side seams together. With the sewing needle and thread, backstitch the side seams together; leave approximately 7"/18 cm unseamed at the bottom hem. You can also use a sewing machine to assemble the pullover.

Fold the Sleeves with the right sides facing each other. With the sewing needle and thread, sew together the sleeve seams using backstitch; leave approximately 7"/18 cm unseamed at the wrist. Pin the Sleeves into the armholes and shoulder seams. Make sure you pin the Sleeves evenly to avoid any bunching or stretching. With the sewing needle and thread, sew the Sleeves into the armholes.

COLLAR

Either continue to maintain the stripe patterns or work the collar as a single color. With either yarn A or yarn B (your choice), pick up 56 (56, 60, 60) stitches from the Back stitch holder, 18 (18, 20, 20) stitches from the left Sleeve stitch holder, 56 (56, 60, 60) stitches from the Front stitch holder, and 18 (18, 20, 20) stitches from the right Sleeve stitch holder—148 (148, 160, 160) stitches total. Work even in stockinette stitch for 1½"/4 cm. Bind off very loosely to ensure the proper head room.

TIES

With the crochet hook and 4 strands of yarn A, crochet 4 chains approximately 1 yard/1 meter each long. Thread one of the chains through the tapestry needle and weave this chain like a shoelace along the left side seam slit of the pullover (see photograph for placement). Repeat for the right side seam slit and the two wrist slits.

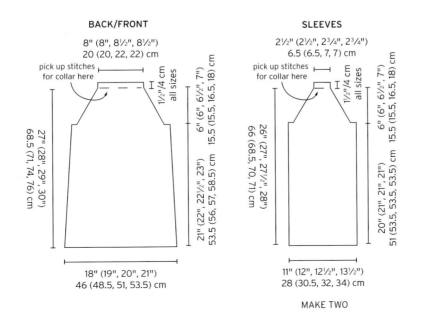

BACK/FRONT

8" (8", 8½", 8½")
20 (20, 22, 22) cm

pick up stitches for collar here

1½"/4 cm all sizes

27" (28", 29", 30")
68.5 (71, 74, 76) cm

6" (6", 6½", 7")
15.5 (15.5, 16.5, 18) cm

21" (22", 22½", 23")
53.5 (56, 57, 58.5) cm

18" (19", 20", 21")
46 (48.5, 51, 53.5) cm

SLEEVES

2½" (2½", 2¾", 2¾")
6.5 (6.5, 7, 7) cm

pick up stitches for collar here

1½"/4 cm all sizes

26" (27", 27½", 28")
66 (68.5, 70, 71) cm

6" (6", 6½", 7")
15.5 (15.5, 16.5, 18) cm

20" (21", 21", 21")
51 (53.5, 53.5, 53.5) cm

11" (12", 12½", 13½")
28 (30.5, 32, 34) cm

MAKE TWO

zippered sweater

I HAVE ALWAYS BEEN A FAN OF ASYMMETRICAL SHAPES AND OFF-CENTER DETAILS. HERE, AN OFF-CENTERED BLACK ZIPPER STANDS OUT ON A BEAUTIFUL, BRIGHT RED, RIBBED-NECK CARDIGAN SWEATER. THE COLLAR SPREADS OUT AS YOU UNZIP THE TOP PART.

4

SIZES
SMALL (MEDIUM, LARGE, EXTRA-LARGE)

FINISHED MEASUREMENTS
CHEST: 38" (40", 42", 44")/96.5 (101.5, 106.5, 112) CM
LENGTH: 22" (23", 23½", 24½")/56 (58.5, 59.5, 62) CM
(NOT INCLUDING COLLAR)

YARN
10 (10, 11, 12) SKEINS SUSS SNUGGLE (60% COTTON/
40% ACRYLIC; 2 OUNCES/57 GRAMS; 126 YARDS/
115 METERS), COLOR FEVER

NOTIONS
1 PAIR SIZE 8 (5 MM) NEEDLES
1 TAPESTRY NEEDLE
SEWING PINS
TWO 4"/10 CM BLACK ANTIQUE JACKET ZIPPERS
ONE 22"/56 CM BLACK ANTIQUE JACKET ZIPPER
SEWING NEEDLE AND RED THREAD

GAUGE
18 STITCHES AND 24 ROWS = 4"/10 CM IN
STOCKINETTE STITCH

TWO-BY-TWO RIB STITCH PATTERN

(with a multiple of 4 plus 2)

Row 1: *Knit 2, purl 2*, repeat from * to * until 2 stitches remain, knit 2.

Row 2: Knit all knit stitches and purl all purl stitches.

Repeat Row 2.

BACK

Cast on 76 (82, 86, 90) stitches. Work in stockinette stitch (knit all right-side rows and purl all wrong-side rows). Increase 1 stitch at the beginning and end of every 22 (22, 22, 24) rows 4 times—84 (90, 94, 98) stitches. Work even until the piece measures 15" (15½", 16", 16½")/ 38 (39.5, 40.5, 42) cm.

ARMHOLE SHAPING

Cast on 8 stitches at the beginning of the next 2 rows—100 (106, 110, 114) stitches total. To cast on new stitches, insert the right-hand needle into the space between the first 2 stitches on the left-hand needle. Pull the yarn through, making a loop, and place that loop back on the left-hand needle. Repeat until you have added the desired number of stitches. Work even until the piece measures 6" (6½", 6½", 7")/15 (16.5, 16.5, 18) cm from armhole shaping.

SHOULDER SHAPING

Bind off 11 (12, 12, 14) stitches at the beginning of the next 2 (4, 6, 2) rows—78 (58, 38, 86) stitches remain. Bind off 10 (10, 0, 12) stitches at the beginning of the next 4 (2, 0, 4) rows—38 (38, 38, 38) stitches remain.

Work in two-by-two rib stitch until collar measures 4½"/11.5 cm from shoulders. Bind off loosely in rib pattern.

LEFT FRONT

Cast on 33 (36, 36, 40) stitches. Work in stockinette stitch with different shaping on the center front and the side seam edge (see diagram).

On the center front edge, increase 1 stitch every 4 rows 32 (32, 34, 32) times. Work even until collar.

At the same time, on the side seam edge, (the right edge when the right side of the piece is facing you), increase 1 stitch every 22 (22, 22, 24) rows 4 times. Work even until the piece measures 15" (15½", 16", 16½")/38 (39.5, 40.5, 42) cm, ending with a wrong-side row.

ARMHOLE SHAPING

Cast on 8 stitches at the beginning of the next right-side row. Work even until the piece measures 6" (6½", 6½", 7")/15 (16.5, 16.5, 18) cm from armhole shaping.

SHOULDER SHAPING

Bind off 11 (12, 12, 14) stitches at the beginning of the next 1 (2, 3, 1) alternate row(s). Bind off 10 (10, 0, 12) stitches at the beginning of the next 2 (1, 0, 2) alternate row(s)—46 stitches remain.

Work even in two-by-two rib stitch until the collar measures 4½"/11.5 cm. Bind off loosely in rib pattern.

RIGHT FRONT

Cast on 64 (64, 66, 70) stitches. Work in stockinette stitch with different shaping on the center front and the side seam edge (see diagram).

On the center front edge (the right edge when the right side of the piece is facing you), work even until bind-off.

At the same time, on the side seam edge (the left edge when the right side of the piece is facing you), increase 1 stitch every 22 (22, 22, 24) rows 4 times—68 (68, 70, 74) stitches total. Work even until the piece measures 15½" (15½", 16", 16½")/39.5 (39.5, 40.5, 42) cm, ending with a right-side row.

ARMHOLE SHAPING

Cast on 8 stitches at the beginning of the next wrong-side row—76 (76, 78, 82) stitches total. Work even until the piece measures 6" (6½", 6½", 7")/15 (16.5, 16.5, 18) cm from armhole shaping.

SHOULDER SHAPING

Bind off 12 (12, 12, 14) stitches at the beginning of the next 2 (2, 3, 1) alternate row(s)—52 (52, 42, 68) stitches total. Bind off 10 (10, 0, 12) stitches at the beginning of the next 1 (1, 0, 2) alternate rows—42 (42, 42, 44) stitches remain.

Work even in two-by-two rib stitch until collar measures 4½"/11.5 cm. Bind off loosely in rib pattern.

SLEEVES (Make two)

Cast on 46 (50, 50, 54) stitches. Work even in stockinette stitch for 6" (7", 7", 7")/15 (18, 18, 18) cm. Switch to two-by-two rib stitch and work for 6"/15 cm. Switch back to stockinette stitch and work for 5½" (5½", 6", 6½")/14 (14, 15, 16.5) cm.

At the same time, increase 1 stitch at the beginning and end of every 26 (26, 26, 22) rows 4 (4, 4, 5) times—54 (58, 58, 64) stitches total.

Bind off.

FINISHING

Weave in all loose ends with the tapestry needle.

Pin the shoulder, neck, and side seams together. With the tapestry needle and yarn, sew together the shoulder, neck, and side seams using backstitch.

With the tapestry needle and yarn, sew the sleeve seams using backstitch, leaving 4"/10 cm at the wrist unseamed. Pin the Sleeves into place at the armholes and, with the tapestry needle and yarn, sew them into the armholes using backstitch.

ZIPPERS

Pin one of the 4"/10 cm zippers into place at one of the wrist slits with the *wrong side* of the zipper on the outside of the garment (see photograph). With the sewing needle and thread, whipstitch the zipper to the Sleeve. Repeat for the second Sleeve.

Lay the sweater flat with the Right Front on top of the Left Front. With a sewing pin, mark the spot on the top of the collar (bind-off edge) where the Right Front collar edge lies on the Left Front collar. Pin the 22"/56 cm zipper into place, starting at the top of the Left Front collar and going down the front of the garment in a straight vertical line. Use the line of knitted stitches to guide you as you pin the zipper in a straight line. Use a sewing machine or the sewing needle and thread to attach the zipper securely.

Starting at the top of the Right Front collar, pin the other half of the zipper along the straight center front edge of the Right Front. With a sewing machine or a sewing needle and thread, attach the zipper to the *wrong side* of the Right Front. Make sure that the knitted piece is attached very closely to the zipper's teeth.

BACK

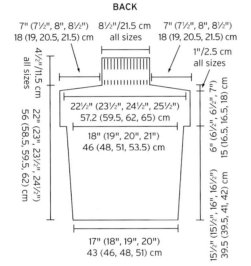

7" (7½", 8", 8½")
18 (19, 20.5, 21.5) cm

8½"/21.5 cm
all sizes

7" (7½", 8", 8½")
18 (19, 20.5, 21.5) cm

1"/2.5 cm
all sizes

4½"/11.5 cm
all sizes

22½" (23½", 24½", 25½")
57.2 (59.5, 62, 65) cm

18" (19", 20", 21")
46 (48, 51, 53.5) cm

6" (6½", 6½", 7")
15 (16.5, 16.5, 18) cm

22" (23", 23½", 24½")
56 (58.5, 59.5, 62) cm

17" (18", 19", 20")
43 (46, 48, 51) cm

15½" (15½", 16", 16½")
39.5 (39.5, 41, 42) cm

SLEEVE

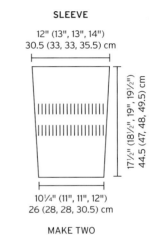

12" (13", 13", 14")
30.5 (33, 33, 35.5) cm

17½" (18½", 19", 19½")
44.5 (47, 48, 49.5) cm

10¼" (11", 11", 12")
26 (28, 28, 30.5) cm

MAKE TWO

LEFT FRONT

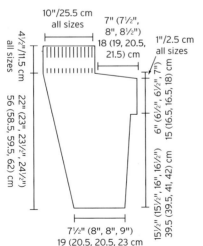

10"/25.5 cm
all sizes

7" (7½", 8", 8½")
18 (19, 20.5, 21.5) cm

1"/2.5 cm
all sizes

4½"/11.5 cm
all sizes

6" (6½", 6½", 7")
15 (16.5, 16.5, 18) cm

22" (23", 23½", 24½")
56 (58.5, 59.5, 62) cm

15½" (15½", 16", 16½")
39.5 (39.5, 41, 42) cm

7½" (8", 8", 9")
19 (20.5, 20.5, 23 cm

RIGHT FRONT

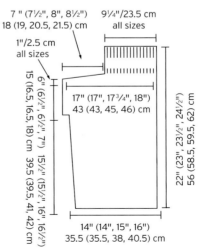

7 " (7½", 8", 8½")
18 (19, 20.5, 21.5) cm

9¼"/23.5 cm
all sizes

1"/2.5 cm
all sizes

6" (6½", 6½", 7")
15 (16.5, 16.5, 18) cm

17" (17", 17¾", 18")
43 (43, 45, 46) cm

22" (23", 23½", 24½") cm
56 (58.5, 59.5, 62) cm

15½" (15½", 16", 16½")
39.5 (39.5, 41, 42) cm

14" (14", 15", 16")
35.5 (35.5, 38, 40.5) cm

tweedy cowl-neck sweater

THIS COWL-NECK PULLOVER IS AS COZY LOOKING AS THOSE EXTRALONG SWEATERS FROM THE MOVIE *FLASHDANCE*. THE TWEEDY EFFECT OF THE TWO-TONAL BLUES EXPLODING INTO SUBTLE, SOFT ALPACA IS A FAVORITE OF MINE. THE OVERSIZED NECK CAN BE PULLED OFF ONE SHOULDER, OR YOU CAN KEEP IT UP HIGH FOR A COMFY LOOK.

SIZES
SMALL (MEDIUM, LARGE)

FINISHED MEASUREMENTS
CHEST: 38" (40", 44")/96.5 (101.5, 112) CM
LENGTH: 28" (29", 30")/71 (73.5, 76) CM

YARN
6 (7, 8) SKEINS SUSS TONAL (53% ACRYLIC/30%
NYLON/17% ALPACA; 1.5 OUNCES/43 GRAMS; 285
YARDS/261 METERS), COLOR BREEZE

NOTIONS
1 PAIR SIZE 11 (8 MM) CIRCULAR NEEDLES, 24"/61 CM
1 LARGE TAPESTRY NEEDLE
SEWING PINS (RECOMMENDED)

GAUGE
11 STITCHES AND 15 ROWS = 4"/10 CM IN STOCKINETTE
STITCH WITH 3 STRANDS OF YARN HELD TOGETHER
12 STITCHES AND 15 ROWS = 4"/10 CM IN TWO-BY-TWO RIB
STITCH WITH 3 STRANDS OF YARN HELD TOGETHER

BACK

Cast on 52 (56, 60) stitches with 3 strands of yarn held together. Work in two-by-two rib stitch (knit 2, purl 2, repeat until the end of the row) until the piece measures 4"/10 cm, ending with a wrong-side row.

Switch to stockinette stitch (knit all right-side rows and purl all wrong-side rows). Work even until the piece measures 21" (22", 22½")/53 (56, 57) cm.

ARMHOLE SHAPING

Cast on 3 stitches at the beginning of the next 2 rows—58 (62, 66) stitches total.

Work even until the piece measures 28" (29", 30")/71 (73.5, 76) cm.

SHOULDER SHAPING AND COLLAR

Bind off 13 (15, 17) stitches at the beginning of the next 2 rows—32 (32, 32) stitches remaining. Switch to two-by-two rib stitch. Increase 1 stitch at the beginning and end of every 2 rows 8 times—48 stitches. Work even in two-by-two rib stitch until piece measures 13"/33 cm from shoulder shaping.

Bind off *loosely* in rib pattern.

FRONT

Work the Front as for the Back.

SLEEVES (Make two)

Cast on 40 (40, 44) stitches loosely with 3 strands of yarn held together. Work in two-by-two rib stitch until the Sleeve measures 4"/10cm, ending with a wrong-side row. Switch to stockinette stitch and work even until the Sleeve measures 18" (19", 19½")/46 (48, 49.5) cm.

Bind off loosely.

FINISHING

Weave in any loose ends with the tapestry needle.

Place the Front and Back pieces together with the right sides facing each other. With the tapestry needle and one strand of yarn A, start at the sleeve edge and backstitch the shoulder and collar seams together. You may find it helpful to pin the two pieces together first. In order to hide the seam when you wear the collar turned over, the first half of the collar should be worked with the right sides facing each other. Turn the garment inside out and resume sewing the collar with the right sides facing out.

With the tapestry needle and two strands of yarn A, sew together the side seams using backstitch. Sew together the sleeve seams using backstitch.

With the tapestry needle and two strands of yarn A, sew the Sleeves into the armholes using backstitch. You may find it helpful to turn the piece inside out and pin the Sleeves into the armholes first. Make sure you pin the Sleeves evenly so that there is no bunching or stretching.

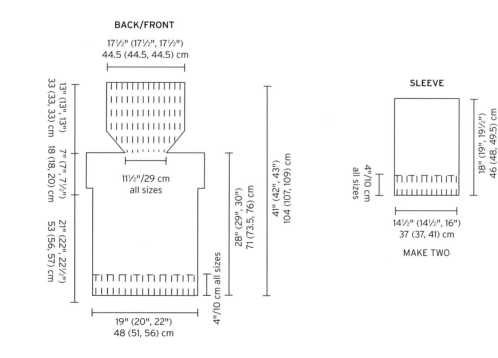

BACK/FRONT

17½" (17½", 17½")
44.5 (44.5, 44.5) cm

13" (13", 13")
33 (33, 33) cm

7" (7", 7½")
18 (18, 20) cm

11½"/29 cm
all sizes

2" (22", 22½")
53 (56, 57) cm

28" (29", 30")
71 (73.5, 76) cm

41" (42", 43")
104 (107, 109) cm

4"/10 cm all sizes

19" (20", 22")
48 (51, 56) cm

SLEEVE

18" (19", 19½")
46 (48, 49.5) cm

4"/10 cm
all sizes

14½" (14½", 16")
37 (37, 41) cm

MAKE TWO

asymmetrical buttoned sweater

KEEP THIS INTERESTING SWEATER BUTTONED UP AT ALL TIMES TO SHOW OFF ITS UNUSUAL DESIGN. CHOCOLATE-BROWN LEATHER BUTTONS DECORATE THE SLEEVES AND RUN UP THE FRONT TO A FUNNEL NECK. I THINK IT LOOKS FUTURISTIC AND CLEAN, LIKE SOMETHING OUT OF THE MOVIE *ESCAPE FROM NEW YORK*. ALTHOUGH IT'S KNIT IN A BASIC STOCKINETTE, THE COLOR AND TEXTURE OF THIS SOFT WOOL MAKE IT UNIQUE.

3

SIZES
SMALL (MEDIUM, LARGE)

FINISHED MEASUREMENTS
CHEST: 37" (39", 41")/94 (99, 104) CM
LENGTH: 20" (21", 22")/51 (53.5, 56) CM (NOT
    INCLUDING COLLAR)

YARN
8 (8, 9) SKEINS SUSS ULL (100% WOOL; 2 OUNCES/
    57 GRAMS; 215 YARDS/197 METERS), COLOR ASH

NOTIONS
1 PAIR SIZE 10 (6 MM) CIRCULAR NEEDLES, 24"/61 CM LONG
1 KNITTING ROW COUNTER (RECOMMENDED)

1 LARGE TAPESTRY NEEDLE
SEWING PINS
13 BROWN SHANK LEATHER BUTTONS, 1"/2.5 CM IN DIAMETER
4 BROWN SHANK LEATHER BUTTONS, 3/4"/2 CM IN DIAMETER
SEWING NEEDLE AND THREAD IN COMPLEMENTARY COLOR

GAUGE
16 STITCHES AND 20 ROWS = 4"/10 CM IN STOCKINETTE
    STITCH WITH TWO STRANDS HELD TOGETHER
22 STITCHES AND 20 ROWS = 4"/10 CM IN TWO-BY-TWO RIB
    STITCH (SLIGHTLY STRETCHED) WITH TWO STRANDS
    HELD TOGETHER (EXACT GAUGE FOR THIS
    MEASUREMENT IS NOT IMPORTANT)

BACK
Cast on 64 (68, 72) stitches with two strands of yarn held together. Work in stockinette stitch (knit all right-side rows and purl all wrong-side rows). Increase 1 stitch at the beginning and end of every 12 rows 5 times—74 (78, 82) stitches total. Work even until the piece measures 13" (13½", 14")/33 (34.5, 35.5) cm from the cast-on edge, ending with a wrong-side row.

ARMHOLE SHAPING
Bind off 4 stitches at the beginning of the next 2 rows—66 (70, 74) stitches total. Decrease 1 stitch at the beginning and end of every right-side row 4 times—58 (62, 66) stitches total. Work even until the piece measures 19" (20", 21")/48 (51, 53.5) cm from the cast-on edge, ending with a wrong-side row.

SHOULDER SHAPING
Bind off 7 (8, 9) stitches at the beginning of the next 4 rows—30 stitches total.

COLLAR
Work even for another 4"/10 cm, or approximately 20 rows. Bind off *loosely*.

LEFT FRONT
Cast on 48 (50, 52) stitches with two strands of yarn held together. Work in stockinette stitch. The Left Front is worked with shaping on both side edges. When the right side (the knit side) of the piece is facing you, the side seam edge is the left-side edge and the button placket edge is the right-side edge.

On the side seam edge, increase 1 stitch every 12 rows 5 times. Work even until the piece measures 13" (13½", 14")/33 (34.5, 35.5) cm from the cast-on edge, ending with a wrong-side row. To shape armhole, bind off 4 stitches at the beginning of the next (right-side) row. Decrease 1 stitch every right-side row 4 times. Work even until the piece measures 19" (20", 21")/48 (51, 53.5) cm from the cast-on edge, ending with a wrong-side row. To shape shoulders, bind off 7 (8, 9) stitches at the beginning of the next 2 right-side rows.

At the same time, on the button band edge, decrease 1 stitch every 5 rows 19 times. Work even until you have completed shoulder shaping on the side seam edge—12 stitches remain.

COLLAR
Work even for another 4"/10cm, or approximately 20 rows. Bind off *loosely*.

RIGHT FRONT
Cast on 12 (14, 16) stitches with two strands of yarn held together. Work in stockinette stitch. The Right Front is worked with shaping on both side edges. When the right side (the knit side) of the piece is facing you, the side seam edge is the right-side edge and the buttonhole placket edge is the left-side edge.

On the side seam edge, increase 1 stitch every 12 rows 5 times. Work even until the piece measures 13" (13½", 14")/33 (34.5, 35.5) cm from the cast-on edge. To shape armhole, bind off 4 stitches at the beginning of the next wrong-side row. Decrease 1 stitch every wrong-side row 4 times. Work even until the piece measures 19" (20", 21")/48 (51, 53.5) cm from the cast-on edge. To shape shoulders, bind off 7 (8, 9) stitches at the beginning of the next 2 wrong-side rows.

At the same time, on the button band edge, increase 1 stitch every 5 (6, 6) rows 17 times. Work even until you have completed the shoulder shaping on the side seam edge—12 stitches remain.

COLLAR

Work even for another 4"/10 cm, or approximately 20 rows. Bind off *loosely.*

SLEEVES
(Make two)

Cast on 40 (42, 44) stitches with two strands of yarn held together. Work even in stockinette stitch until the piece measures 5"/12.5 cm from the cast-on edge. Increase 1 stitch at the beginning and end of every 14 (15, 13) rows 5 (5, 6) times—50 (52, 56) stitches total. Work even until the piece measures 20" (21", 21½")/51 (53.5, 54.5) cm from the cast-on edge, ending with a wrong-side row.

To shape sleeve cap, bind off 4 stitches at the beginning of the next 2 rows—42 (44, 48) stitches total. Decrease 1 stitch at the beginning and end of every right-side row 7 times—28 (30, 34) stitches total. Decrease 1 stitch at the beginning and end of every row 3 times—22 (24, 28) stitches total.

Bind off.

BACK

7½"/19 cm all sizes

3½" (4", 4½")
9 (10, 11.5) cm

4"/10 cm all sizes

18½" (19½", 20½")
47 (49.5, 52) cm

6" (6½", 7")
15 (16.5, 18) cm

13" (13½", 14")
33 (34, 35.5) cm

20" (21", 22")
51 (53.5, 56) cm

16" (17", 18")
40.5 (43, 46) cm

LEFT FRONT

3"/7.5 cm
all sizes

3½" (4", 4½")
9 (10, 11.5) cm

4"/10 cm all sizes

20" (21", 22")
51 (53.5, 56) cm

6" (6½", 7")
15 (16.5, 18) cm

13" (13½", 14")
33 (34, 35.5) cm

12" (12½", 13")
30.5 (32, 33) cm

FINISHING	Weave in all loose ends with the tapestry needle.
	Note: All lapels and sleeve cuffs are worked with two strands of yarn held together.
BUTTON BAND	Starting at the bottom hem of the Left Front, pick up 128 (136, 144) stitches along the Left Front band edge. Work in two-by-two rib stitch (knit 2, purl 2, repeat until the end of the row) for 12 rows. Bind off in rib pattern.
BUTTONHOLE BAND	Starting at the bottom hem of the Right Front, pick up 128 (136, 144) stitches along the Right Front band edge. Work in two-by-two rib stitch for 6 rows.
	Start at the top of the collar and work an eyelet row (while maintaining two-by-two rib stitch) as follows:
	Work 3 (3, 4) stitches, yarn over, work 2 stitches together, (work 4 stitches, yarn over, work 2 stitches together) 3 times, [work 12 (13, 14) stitches, yarn over, work 2 together] 7 times, work remaining 7 (8, 8) stitches.
	Work 5 rows in two-by-two rib stitch. Bind off in rib pattern.
	Pin together the shoulder seams and side seams. With the tapestry needle and two strands of yarn, sew together the shoulder seams and side seams using backstitch.
LEFT SLEEVE	With right side facing you, start at the cast-on (wrist) edge of the Sleeve and pick up 24 stitches along the *right side* of the 5"/12.5 cm straight edge (see Sleeve diagram). Work in a two-by-two rib pattern for 3 rows.
	Work an eyelet row (while maintaining two-by-two rib stitch) as follows:
	Work 4 stitches, yarn over, work 2 stitches together, (work 5 stitches, yarn over, work 2 stitches together) twice, work 4 stitches.
	Work 3 rows in two-by-two rib stitch pattern. Bind off in rib pattern.
RIGHT SLEEVE	With right side facing you, start at the cast-on (wrist) edge of the Sleeve and pick up 24 stitches along the *left side* of the 5"/12.5 cm straight edge (see Sleeve diagram). Work in a two-by-two rib pattern as for left Sleeve.
BOTH SLEEVES	With the tapestry needle and two strands of yarn, sew the sleeve seams together using backstitch. Leave the last 5"/12.5 cm near the wrist unseamed. At the top of the cuff slit, tack down the narrow edge of the ribbed buttonhole band on the right side of the Sleeve with small whipstitches.
	With the tapestry needle and two strands of yarn, attach the Sleeves to the armholes. You may find it helpful to pin the Sleeves into place first.
BUTTONS	Place the pullover right-side up with the Right Front buttonhole band over the Left Front button band. Line up the collar and bottom hem. Use the yarn over buttonholes to find where the buttons should be placed, and mark those spots with sewing pins.
	With the sewing needle and thread, attach the 4 smaller buttons to the collar of the pullover at the spots indicated by the sewing pins. Attach 7 of the larger buttons to the band at the spots indicated by the pins.
	With the same method, use sewing pins to mark where the buttons should be attached to the sleeve cuffs. With the sewing needle and thread, attach 3 of the larger buttons to each cuff.

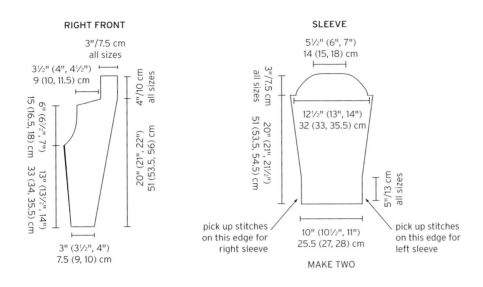

RIGHT FRONT

3"/7.5 cm
all sizes

3½" (4", 4½")
9 (10, 11.5) cm

4"/10 cm
all sizes

6" (6½", 7")
15 (16.5, 18) cm

20" (21", 22")
51 (53.5, 56) cm

13" (13½", 14")
33 (34, 35.5) cm

3" (3½", 4")
7.5 (9, 10) cm

SLEEVE

5½" (6", 7")
14 (15, 18) cm

3"/7.5 cm
all sizes

20" (21", 21½")
51 (53.5, 54.5) cm

12½" (13", 14")
32 (33, 35.5) cm

5"/13 cm
all sizes

pick up stitches
on this edge for
right sleeve

10" (10½", 11")
25.5 (27, 28) cm

pick up stitches
on this edge for
left sleeve

MAKE TWO

open-front pullover

A FEW YEARS AGO, I DESIGNED A SWEATER FOR AN ACTOR WHO NEEDED TO GET IN AND OUT OF HER COSTUME QUICKLY. THIS PULLOVER, WITH ITS CLEVER OPENING FROM THE COLLARBONE DOWN, EVOLVED FROM THAT DESIGN. BECAUSE OF THE FRONT SLIT AND THE BELL-SHAPED SLEEVES, YOU CAN MOVE VERY EASILY IN THIS SWEATER—JUST THE PIECE YOU'LL REACH FOR ON WEEKENDS.

SIZES
SMALL (MEDIUM, LARGE)

FINISHED MEASUREMENTS
CHEST: 36" (38", 40")/91.5 (96.5, 101.5) CM
LENGTH: 33" (34", 35")/84 (86.5, 89) CM

YARN
11 (12, 12) SKEINS SUSS CRUNCH (70% COTTON/20%
   ACRYLIC/8% NYLON/2% ALPACA; 2 OUNCES/57 GRAMS;
   153 YARDS/140 METERS), COLOR ASH

NOTIONS
1 PAIR SIZE 9 (5.5 MM) CIRCULAR NEEDLES, 24"/61 CM LONG
1 CABLE NEEDLE
1 LARGE TAPESTRY NEEDLE
SEWING PINS
1 SIZE G (4 MM) CROCHET HOOK

GAUGE
16 STITCHES AND 20 ROWS = 4"/10 CM IN REVERSE
   STOCKINETTE STITCH
20 STITCHES AND 20 ROWS = 4"/10 CM IN TWO-BY-TWO
   RIB STITCH

CABLE-10 PATTERN

Rows 1 and 3: Knit 2, purl 4, knit 4, purl 4, knit 2—16 stitches total.

Rows 2 and 4: Purl 2, knit 4, purl 4, knit 4, purl 2.

Row 5: Knit 2, purl 4, slip the next 2 stitches onto a cable needle and hold *in front of* the work, knit the next 2 stitches from the left-hand needle, knit 2 stitches from the cable needle, purl 4, knit 2.

Rows 6, 8, and 10: Purl 2, knit 4, purl 4, knit 4, purl 2.

Rows 7 and 9: Knit 2, purl 4, knit 4, purl 4, knit 2.

Repeat Rows 1–10.

BACK

Cast on 80 (84, 88) stitches. Work in reverse stockinette (purl all right-side rows and knit all wrong-side rows) for 32 (34, 36) stitches, cable 10 (16 stitches total), work in reverse stockinette for 32 (34, 36) stitches. Repeat the cable-10 pattern until collar.

Decrease 1 stitch at the beginning and end of every 10 rows 6 times—68 (72, 76) stitches. Work even until the piece measures 20½" (21", 21½")/52 (53.5, 54.5) cm.

ARMHOLE SHAPING

Bind off 3 stitches at the beginning of the next 2 rows—62 (66, 70) stitches. Decrease 1 stitch at the beginning and end of every other row 5 times—52 (56, 60) stitches. Work even until the piece measures 26" (27", 28")/66 (68.5, 71) cm.

COLLAR

Bind off 4 stitches at the beginning of the next 6 rows—28 (32, 36) stitches.

Work in two-by-two rib stitch (knit 2 stitches, purl 2 stitches, repeat until the end of the row) until collar measures 6"/15 cm, or approximately 30 rows. Bind off *loosely* to ensure sufficient head room.

LEFT FRONT

Cast on 46 (48, 50) stitches. Work in reverse stockinette stitch for 12 (14, 16) stitches, cable 10 (16 stitches total), work in reverse stockinette stitch for 18 stitches. Maintain the cable-10 pattern until bind-off.

Decrease 1 stitch at the beginning of every 5th right-side row 10 times—36 (38, 40) stitches.

To shape armhole, bind off 3 stitches at the beginning of the next right-side row—33 (35, 37) stitches. Decrease 1 stitch at the beginning of every right-side row 5 times—28 (30, 32) stitches.

When the piece measures 24" (25", 26")/61 (63.5, 66) cm, bind off 8 stitches at the beginning of the next wrong-side row to shape neckline. Decrease 1 stitch at neckline edge for 2 (4, 6) rows. Decrease 1 stitch on every wrong-side row 2 (4, 6) times.

At the same time, work even on armhole edge until the piece measures 26" (27", 28")/66 (68.5, 71) cm. Bind off 4 stitches at the beginning of the next 3 right-side rows.

RIGHT FRONT

Cast on 46 (48, 50) stitches. Work in reverse stockinette stitch for 18 stitches, cable 10 (16 stitches total), work in reverse stockinette stitch for 12 (14, 16) stitches. Maintain the cable-10 pattern until bind-off.

Decrease 1 stitch at the beginning of every 5th wrong-side row 10 times—36 (38, 40) stitches.

To shape armhole, bind off 3 stitches at the beginning of the next wrong-side row—33 (35, 37) stitches. Decrease 1 stitch at the beginning of every wrong-side row 5 times—28 (30, 32) stitches.

When the piece measures 24" (25", 26")/61 (63.5, 66) cm, bind off 8 stitches at the beginning of the next right-side row to shape neckline. Decrease 1 stitch at neckline edge for 2 (4, 6) rows. Decrease 1 stitch on every right-side row 2 (4, 6) times.

At the same time, work even on armhole edge until the piece measures 26" (27", 28")/66 (68.5, 71) cm. Bind off 4 stitches at the beginning of the next 3 wrong-side rows.

SLEEVES (Make two)

Cast on 74 (76, 80) stitches. Work 29 (30, 32) stitches in reverse stockinette stitch, cable 10 (16 stitches total), work 29 (30, 32) stitches in reverse stockinette stitch. Maintain the cable-10 pattern until bind-off. Decrease 1 stitch at the beginning and end of every 6 (7, 7) rows 15 (14, 14) times—44 (48, 52) stitches. Work even until the piece measures 19½" (20½", 21")/49.5 (52, 53.5) cm, or approximately 98 (102, 105) rows.

Bind off 3 stitches at the beginning of the next 2 rows—38 (42, 46) stitches. Decrease 1 stitch at the beginning and end of every 3 rows 6 times—26 (30, 34) stitches. Decrease 1 stitch and the beginning and end of every row for 3 (3, 4) rows—20 (24, 26) stitches.

Bind off.

FINISHING

Place the Right Front and Left Front pieces side by side with the right sides facing up (see diagram). Pin the top neckline edges together to hold the pieces in place while you work the collar. Pick up 20 stitches along the right collar edge and 20 stitches along the left collar edge—40 stitches total. When transitioning from the right collar to the left, pull the stitches tight and remove pins as you work. Work in two-by-two rib stitch until collar measures 6"/15 cm, or approximately 30 rows, from shoulder. Bind off *loosely* to ensure sufficient room to pull the sweater over your head.

Weave in all loose ends with the tapestry needle.

Place the Right Front and Back pieces together with the right sides facing each other and the shoulders lined up. Pin them together. With the tapestry needle and yarn, sew the shoulder seams together using backstitch. Do the same for the Left Front. Sew the side seams using backstitch.

Pin the sleeve seams and use the tapestry needle and yarn to sew using backstitch. Pin the Sleeves into the armholes following the contours of the cap shaping. You may find it helpful to turn the piece inside out to do this. Sew the Sleeves into the armholes.

With the crochet hook and yarn, start at the bottom hem of the Right Front and work a row of double crochet along the slit opening of the pullover. When you reach the top point of the "V" (where the Right and Left Fronts meet), turn and work a row of double crochet along the Left Front slit opening.

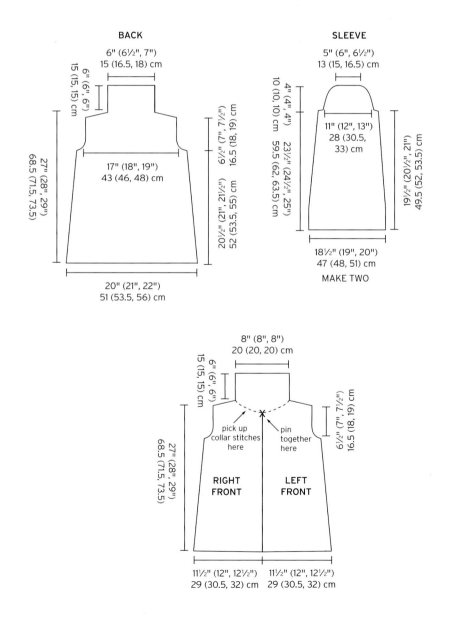

BACK

6" (6½", 7")
15 (16.5, 18) cm

6" (6", 6") 15 (15, 15) cm

6½" (7", 7½") 16.5 (18, 19) cm

17" (18", 19")
43 (46, 48) cm

27" (28", 29") 68.5 (71.5, 73.5)

20½" (21", 21½") 52 (53.5, 55) cm

20" (21", 22")
51 (53.5, 56) cm

SLEEVE

5" (6", 6½")
13 (15, 16.5) cm

4" (4", 4") 10 (10, 10) cm

23½" (24½", 25") 59.5 (62, 63.5) cm

11" (12", 13")
28 (30.5, 33) cm

19½" (20½", 21") 49.5 (52, 53.5) cm

18½" (19", 20")
47 (48, 51) cm

MAKE TWO

8" (8", 8")
20 (20, 20) cm

6" (6", 6") 15 (15, 15) cm

6½" (7", 7½") 16.5 (18, 19) cm

pick up collar stitches here

pin together here

27" (28", 29") 68.5 (71.5, 73.5)

RIGHT FRONT

LEFT FRONT

11½" (12", 12½")
29 (30.5, 32) cm

11½" (12", 12½")
29 (30.5, 32) cm

dip-dyed raglan pullover

TRULY A CUSTOMIZED SWEATER, THIS PIECE IS FIRST KNIT IN STOCKINETTE. THEN YOU TURN THE PURL SIDE OUT AND CLOSE THE SEAMS ON THE OUTSIDE AS A DECORATIVE DETAIL. I DIP-DYED THE ENDS OF THE SLEEVES AND THE BOTTOM IN BLACK DYE, WHICH COMES OUT GRAY AND REMINDS ME OF BIRCH TREES IN WINTERTIME. YOU COULD TRY OTHER COLORS WITH A NEUTRAL-COLORED YARN. THE BOATNECK AND LONG BODY ARE VERY ATTRACTIVE.

4

SIZES
SMALL (MEDIUM, LARGE)

FINISHED MEASUREMENTS
CHEST: 34" (36", 38")/86.5 (91.5, 96.5) CM
LENGTH: 26" (27", 28")/66 (68.5, 71) CM

YARN
8 (9, 9) SKEINS SUSS NUBBY (100% COTTON; 1.5 OUNCES/
43 GRAMS; 135 YARDS/123 METERS), COLOR NATURAL

NOTIONS
1 PAIR SIZE 6 (4 MM) NEEDLES
SEWING PINS
1 TAPESTRY NEEDLE
1 PACKAGE RIT FABRIC DYE, BLACK
1 LARGE STAINLESS STEEL BOWL (OR STAINLESS
    STEEL SINK)
1 PAIR RUBBER GLOVES

GAUGE
20 STITCHES AND 24 ROWS = 4"/10 CM IN
    STOCKINETTE STITCH

BACK

Cast on 84 (88, 94) stitches. Work even in stockinette stitch (knit all right-side rows and purl all wrong-side rows) until the piece measures 19½" (20", 20½")/49.5 (51, 52) cm, ending with a wrong-side row.

SHOULDER SHAPING

Bind off 4 stitches at the beginning of the next 2 rows—76 (80, 86) stitches. Work 1 row even. Decrease 1 stitch at the beginning and end of every wrong-side row 18 (19, 21) times—40 (42, 44) stitches remain. Work 2 rows even.

Bind off loosely.

FRONT

Work the Front as for the Back.

SLEEVES (Make two)

Cast on 38 (40, 44) stitches. Work in stockinette stitch. Increase 1 stitch at the beginning and end of every 13 (14, 14) rows 9 times—56 (58, 62) stitches total. Work even until the sleeve measures 19½" (21", 21½")/49.5 (53.5, 54.5) cm.

To shape sleeve cap, bind off 4 stitches at the beginning of the next 2 rows—48 (50, 54) stitches. Work 1 row even. Decrease 1 stitch at the beginning and end of every wrong-side row 18 (19, 21) times—12 stitches remain. Work 2 rows even.

Bind off loosely.

FINISHING

Weave in any loose ends with the tapestry needle.

ASSEMBLY

To achieve its "deconstructed" look, this pullover is worn with the purl side facing outward. Work all seams with a ¼"/6 mm seam allowance showing on the *outside* of the piece.

Place the Front and Back pieces together with the *knit sides facing each other.* With the tapestry needle and yarn, backstitch the side seams together. You may find it helpful to pin the two pieces together first.

Fold the Sleeves with the *knit sides facing each other.* With the tapestry needle and yarn, sew together the sleeve seams using backstitch. With the *purl sides facing out,* pin the Sleeves into the shoulder seams. Make sure you pin the Sleeves evenly to avoid any bunching or stretching.

With the tapestry needle and yarn, backstitch the Sleeves to the shoulder seams.

DYEING

In a large stainless steel bowl or sink, dissolve all the powdered dye in the package in cold water with ¼ cup (59 ml) salt. Make sure to use stainless steel. If you spill the dye on any porcelain or tile, use a bleach cleanser to remove stains.

To achieve a faded effect with the dyeing process, dip the garment in the dye 1″/2.5 cm at a time.

Dip approximately 1″/2.5 cm of each Sleeve into the dye. After you dip the Sleeves in the dye, rinse them under water for approximately 2 minutes. Squeeze out any excess water.

Dip approximately 2″/5 cm of each Sleeve into the dye. Rinse in cold water again for approximately 2 minutes and squeeze out the excess water.

Repeat the process, dipping the Sleeves approximately 3″/7.5 cm into the dye this time.

Repeat this gradual dyeing process for the bottom hem of the pullover. Make sure you rinse all the edges thoroughly so that no excess dye remains and bleeds into the rest of the sweater. As you wear and wash the sweater over time, the dye will fade gradually—I love that worn look. Hang the garment on a hanger to dry overnight before wearing.

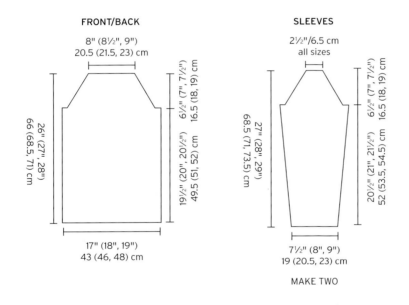

FRONT/BACK

8″ (8½″, 9″)
20.5 (21.5, 23) cm

6½″ (7″, 7½″) 16.5 (18, 19) cm

19½″ (20″, 20½″) 49.5 (51, 52) cm

26″ (27″, 28″) 66 (68.5, 71) cm

17″ (18″, 19″)
43 (46, 48) cm

SLEEVES

2½″/6.5 cm
all sizes

6½″ (7″, 7½″) 16.5 (18, 19) cm

27″ (28″, 29″) 68.5 (71, 73.5) cm

20½″ (21″, 21½″) 52 (53.5, 54.5) cm

7½″ (8″, 9″)
19 (20.5, 23) cm

MAKE TWO

dolman sleeve
open-neck pullover

I LOVE TO KNIT FROM THE BEGINNING OF ONE SLEEVE TO THE END OF THE OTHER SLEEVE—IT JUST SEEMS SO SIMPLE AND SATISFYING. THAT'S HOW YOU MAKE THIS CASUAL DOWNTIME SWEATER: KNITTING THE CANTALOUPE-AND-CHILI-PEPPER YARN SIDEWAYS. THE SILHOUETTE, WHICH IS ROOMY AND HAS A WIDE NECK AND DRAWSTRING WAIST, WAS VERY BIG IN THE EIGHTIES AND IS POPULAR ONCE AGAIN. ITS EASY FIT WORKS FOR MANY SIZES.

SIZES
SMALL (MEDIUM, LARGE)

FINISHED MEASUREMENTS
CHEST: 34" (36", 38")/86.5 (91.5, 96.5) CM
LENGTH: 22½" (23½", 24½")/57 (59.5, 62) CM

YARN
3 (3, 3) SKEINS SUSS TONAL (53% ACRYLIC/30%
   NYLON/17% ALPACA; 1.5 OUNCES/43 GRAMS;
   285 YARDS/261 METERS), COLOR BURST

NOTIONS
1 PAIR SIZE 10 (6 MM) CIRCULAR NEEDLES, 24"/61 CM LONG
1 PAIR SIZE 10 (6 MM) DOUBLE-POINTED NEEDLES
1 LARGE TAPESTRY NEEDLE

GAUGE
16 STITCHES AND 20 ROWS = 4"/10 CM IN
   STOCKINETTE STITCH

BACK

Cast on 20 (20, 22) stitches. Work even in stockinette stitch (knit all right-side rows and purl all wrong-side rows) for 6 rows. Increase 1 stitch at the beginning of the next right-side row—21 (21, 23) stitches total. Increase 1 stitch at the beginning of every 4 right-side rows 9 times—30 (30, 32) stitches total. Work even until the piece measures 18" (18½", 19")/ 46 (47, 48) cm, ending with a wrong-side row.

Increase 1 stitch at the beginning of every right-side row and the end of every wrong-side row for 14 rows—44 (44, 46) stitches total. Increase 1 stitch at the beginning of every right-side row 4 times—48 (48, 50) stitches total.

Cast on 44 (48, 50) stitches at the beginning of the next right-side row—92 (96, 100) stitches total. To cast on new stitches, insert the right-hand needle into the space between the first 2 stitches on the left-hand needle. Pull the yarn through, making a loop, and place that loop back on the left-hand needle. Repeat until you have cast on the desired numbers of stitches.

Work even until the piece measures 25" (26", 26½")/63.5 (66, 67.5) cm from the cast-on edge.

To shape neckline, decrease 1 stitch at the beginning of the next 3 wrong-side rows—89 (93, 97) stitches total. Work even until the piece measures 36½" (37½", 39")/93 (95, 99) cm from the cast-on edge. Increase 1 stitch at the beginning of the next 3 wrong-side rows— 92 (96, 100) stitches total.

Work even until the piece measures 39½" (41", 42½")/100 (104, 108) cm from the cast-on edge, ending with a wrong-side row. Bind off 44 (48, 50) stitches at the beginning of the next (right-side) row—48 (48, 50) stitches total.

Decrease 1 stitch at the beginning of every right-side row 4 times—44 (44, 46) stitches total. Decrease 1 stitch at the beginning of every right-side row and at the end of every wrong-side row for 14 rows—30 (30, 32) stitches total. Work even until the piece measures 44" (45½", 47")/112 (115.5, 119.5) cm.

Decrease 1 stitch at the beginning of the next right-side row—29 (29, 31) stitches total. Decrease 1 stitch at the beginning of every 4 right-side rows 9 times—20 (20, 22) stitches total. Work even for 6 rows.

Bind off loosely.

FRONT

Work the Front as for the Back.

DRAWSTRING Cast on 4 stitches on one of the double-pointed needles.

Make an I-cord as follows: Knit 4. With the right side facing you, slide these stitches from the left end of the double-pointed needle to the right end and switch this needle to your left hand. The right needle has now become the left needle. Bringing the working yarn around the back, knit the 4 stitches. Repeat until you have an I-cord that measures 72"/183 cm from the cast-on edge.

Bind off.

FINISHING Weave in all loose ends with the tapestry needle.

Place the two knitted pieces together with right sides facing each other. With the tapestry needle and yarn, sew together the seams from the neckline shaping to the wrists using backstitch. Use small stitches and a narrow seam allowance so the seam is not too obvious along the top of the shoulder and arm. You may find it helpful to pin the pieces together first.

With the tapestry needle and yarn, sew together the seams from the wrists to the bottom hem. Leave 1"/2.5 cm unseamed at the bottom hem.

DRAWSTRING To make the drawstring channel, fold over ½"/13 mm of the bottom hem toward the wrong side of the pullover. With the tapestry needle and yarn, whipstitch this channel to the wrong side of the pullover, making sure that you leave openings at the right side seam to thread the Drawstring through.

Tie knots at both ends of the I-cord Drawstring and thread it through the channel. Try on your new sweater, pull the I-cord to the desired width, and tie it in a bow.

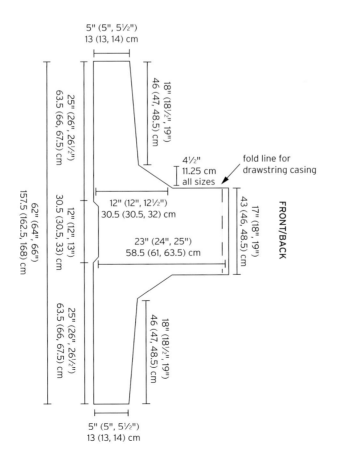

separates

golden evening top

THE RUCHING DETAIL ON THE SIDE MEANS YOU CAN WEAR THIS TOP LONG, AS SHOWN HERE, OR PULL IT UP SHORT ENOUGH TO SHOW SOME MIDRIFF. KNIT MAINLY IN TINY STOCKINETTE, THE GOLD-COLORED BAMBOO YARN SPARKLES JUST ENOUGH TO ATTRACT SOME ATTENTION. THE SLEEVELESS SHAPE, FUNNEL NECK, AND OPENWORK PATTERN ALL ADD A TOUCH OF ELEGANCE.

SIZES
SMALL (MEDIUM, LARGE)

FINISHED MEASUREMENTS
CHEST: 30" (32", 34")/76 (81, 86.5) CM
LENGTH: 25" (26", 27")/63.5 (66, 68.5) CM (NOT INCLUDING COLLAR)

YARN
A: 5 (5, 6) SKEINS SUSS BAMBOO (100% BAMBOO;
1 OUNCE/28 GRAMS; 126 YARDS/115 METERS), COLOR GOLDEN WHEAT
B: 5 (5, 6) SKEINS SUSS SHINE (100% VISCOSE; 1 OUNCE/ 28 GRAMS; 136 YARDS/124 METERS), COLOR BEIGE

NOTIONS
1 PAIR SIZE 7 (4.5 MM) NEEDLES
1 PAIR SIZE 7 (4.5 MM) DOUBLE-POINTED NEEDLES
TAPESTRY NEEDLE
SEWING NEEDLE AND THREAD IN COMPLEMENTARY COLOR

GAUGE
22 STITCHES AND 26 ROWS = 4"/10 CM IN STOCKINETTE STITCH

EYELET PATTERN

Rows 1 and 5: *Knit 3, yarn over, knit 2 together*, repeat from * to * until the end of the row.

Rows 2 and 4: Purl all stitches.

Row 3: Knit 1, *yarn over, knit 2 stitches together, knit 3*, repeat from * to * until the end of the row.

BACK

Cast on 82 (88, 94) stitches with yarn A and yarn B held together. Work in stockinette stitch (knit all right-side rows and purl all wrong-side rows) until the piece measures 18" (18½", 19")/46 (47, 48.5) cm from the cast-on edge, ending with a wrong-side row.

ARMHOLE SHAPING

Decrease 1 stitch at the beginning and end of the next 8 rows—66 (72, 78) stitches. Decrease 1 stitch at the beginning and end of every other row 5 times—56 (62, 68) stitches. Decrease 1 stitch at the beginning and end of every 4 rows 4 (5, 6) times—48 (52, 56) stitches. Work even until the piece measures 25" (26", 27")/63.5, 66, 68.5) cm.

SHOULDER SHAPING

Bind off 5 (7, 7) stitches at the beginning of the next 2 rows—38 (38, 42) stitches remain.

Work even for 12 rows. Bind off loosely.

FRONT

Work the Front as for the Back except for eyelet pattern. Maintain the shaping as for the Back.

When the piece measures 19" (19½", 20")/48 (49.5, 51) cm from the cast-on edge, ending with a wrong-side row, work eyelet pattern once.

CHANNEL FOR TIE

Cast on 9 stitches with one strand of yarn A and one strand of yarn B held together. Work in stockinette stitch until the piece measures 14"/35.5 cm. Bind off.

TIE

Cast on 4 stitches on one of the double-pointed needles with one strand of yarn A and one strand of yarn B held together.

Make an I-cord as follows: Knit 4. Switch the needles in your hands; the needle with the stitches is on the left again. With the right side facing you, slide the stitches from the left end of the needle to the right end. Bring the working yarn around the back and knit the 4 stitches. Repeat until you have an I-cord that measures 50"/127 cm from the cast-on edge.

Bind off.

FINISHING　　Weave in all loose ends with the tapestry needle.

Place the Front and Back pieces together with the right sides facing each other. With the tapestry needle and yarn A, sew together the shoulder and collar seams using backstitch.

With the tapestry needle and yarn A, sew together the side seams using backstitch.

Starting at the bottom hem, center the Channel over the left side seam with the right side facing out. You may find it helpful to pin it into place before sewing. With the sewing needle and thread, whipstitch the edges of the Channel to the outside of the top. You can also use a sewing machine. Make sure you leave the bottom and top seams open for the Tie.

With the tapestry needle and thread, start at the bottom of the left side seam and work a small running stitch up the center of the Channel, creating two channels (see photograph).

Starting at the bottom, thread the Tie up one channel and down the other. Adjust the Tie to the desired length.

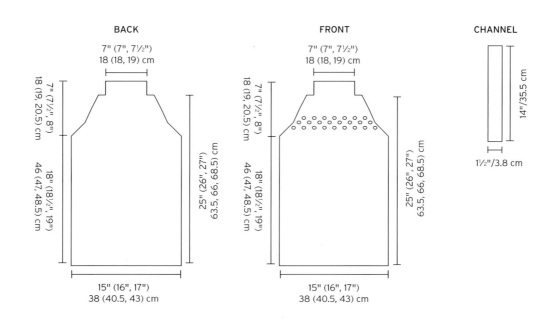

BACK

7" (7", 7½")
18 (18, 19) cm

7" (7½", 8")
18 (19, 20.5) cm

18" (18½", 19")
46 (47, 48.5) cm

25" (26", 27")
63.5, 66, 68.5) cm

15" (16", 17")
38 (40.5, 43) cm

FRONT

7" (7", 7½")
18 (18, 19) cm

7" (7½", 8")
18 (19, 20.5) cm

18" (18½", 19")
46 (47, 48.5) cm

25" (26", 27")
63.5, 66, 68.5) cm

15" (16", 17")
38 (40.5, 43) cm

CHANNEL

14"/35.5 cm

1½"/3.8 cm

button tee

A KNITTED T-SHIRT IS QUITE EYECATCHING, AND I LOVE THE FINE COTTON YARN USED TO CREATE IT. KNITTING ON SMALL NEEDLES WILL TAKE SOME TIME, BUT THE END RESULT IS SO BEAUTIFUL AND YOU CAN WEAR IT WITH ALMOST ANYTHING, FROM DRESSY PANTS TO KHAKIS TO SKIRTS. IT'S ESPECIALLY NICE WITH A LONG, FLOWERY SKIRT AND A PEARL NECKLACE IN THE SUMMER. THE CROCHET LOOPS FOR EACH LITTLE BUTTON ARE A DELICATE TOUCH.

SIZES
SMALL (MEDIUM, LARGE)

FINISHED MEASUREMENTS
CHEST: 35" (37", 39")/89 (94, 99) CM
LENGTH: 25" (26", 27")/63.5 (66, 68.5) CM

YARN
4 (5, 6) SKEINS SUSS PERLE COTTON (100% COTTON;
   2 OUNCES/57 GRAMS; 256 YARDS/234 METERS),
   COLOR LINEN

NOTIONS
1 PAIR SIZE 4 (3.5 MM) NEEDLES
14 ROCK/SHELL BUTTONS, ½"/13 MM IN DIAMETER
   (AVAILABLE AT WW.SUSSDESIGN.COM)
1 SIZE F (3.75 MM) CROCHET HOOK
1 TAPESTRY NEEDLE
SEWING NEEDLE AND THREAD IN COMPLEMENTARY COLOR

GAUGE
24 STITCHES AND 32 ROWS = 4"/10 CM IN STOCKINETTE
   STITCH AND SEED STITCH

SEED STITCH PATTERN

Row 1: *Knit 1, purl 1*, repeat from * to * until the end of the row.

Row 2: *Purl 1, knit 1*, repeat from * to * until the end of the row.

Repeat Rows 1 and 2.

BACK

Cast on 106 (112, 118) stitches. Work in seed stitch for 12 rows total.

Switch to stockinette stitch (knit all right-side rows and purl all wrong-side rows) until the piece measures 18½" (19", 19½")/47 (48, 49.5) cm from the cast-on edge, ending with a wrong-side row.

Bind off 4 stitches at the beginning of the next 2 rows—98 (104, 110) stitches.

Decrease 1 stitch at the beginning and end of the next 24 (25, 27) right-side rows—50 (54, 56) stitches. Work 1 row even.

Bind off.

FRONT

Work the Front as for the Back.

SLEEVES (Make two)

Cast on 64 (68, 72) stitches. Work in seed stitch. Increase 1 stitch at the beginning and end of every wrong-side row 5 times—74 (78, 82) stitches. Work 1 row even.

Bind off 4 stitches at the beginning of the next 2 rows—66 (70, 74) stitches.

Decrease 1 stitch at the beginning and end of the next 24 (25, 27) right-side rows—18 (20, 20) stitches. Work 1 row even.

Bind off in seed stitch pattern.

FINISHING

Weave in all loose ends with the tapestry needle.

Place the Front and Back pieces together with the right sides facing each other. With the tapestry needle and yarn, sew together the right side seam using backstitch. Start at the armhole and sew together the left side seam, leaving the last 7½"/19 cm unseamed.

With the tapestry needle and yarn, sew the sleeve seams using backstitch. Sew the right Sleeve into place using backstitch. Start at the Back neck and sew the left Sleeve into place, leaving the last 5"/12.5 cm of the front shoulder seam unseamed (see photograph).

With the crochet hook and two strands of yarn, start at the hem of the side slit opening and work a single crochet along one edge of the slit, turn, and start working a single crochet along the other edge. Place 8 button loops approximately ¾"/2 cm apart. Create button loops by chaining 8 stitches and then reattaching that loop and continuing the single crochet border.

With the crochet hook and two strands of yarn, work a single crochet along the slit in the shoulder seam. Make 6 buttonhole loops approximately ¾"/2 cm apart.

With the sewing needle and thread, sew on 8 buttons at the side seam opening and 6 buttons at the shoulder seam opening.

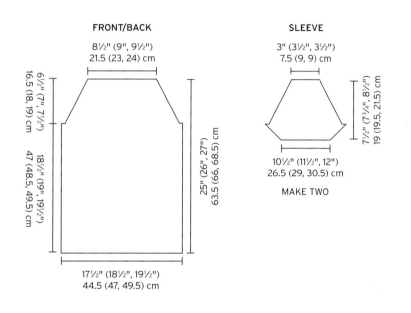

FRONT/BACK

8½" (9", 9½")
21.5 (23, 24) cm

6½" (7", 7½")
16.5 (18, 19) cm

18½" (19", 19½")
47 (48.5, 49.5) cm

25" (26", 27")
63.5 (66, 68.5) cm

17½" (18½", 19½")
44.5 (47, 49.5) cm

SLEEVE

3" (3½", 3½")
7.5 (9, 9) cm

7½" (7¾", 8½")
19 (19.5, 21.5) cm

10½" (11½", 12")
26.5 (29, 30.5) cm

MAKE TWO

cozy hoodie with skirt

THIS IS THE ULTIMATE CASUAL OUTFIT THAT YOU CAN THROW ON AND FORGET ABOUT—IT'S THAT COMFORTABLE. SUSS LOVE IS A SYNTHETIC YARN WITH A CASHMERE FEEL. IT'S INCREDIBLE TO THE TOUCH *AND* IT'S VEGAN. THE PULL-ON DRAWSTRING SKIRT HAS PRETTY POCKETS AND IS CASUAL AND FUN WITH FLIP-FLOPS, WHETHER YOU PAIR IT WITH THE HOODIE OR WEAR IT SEPARATELY.

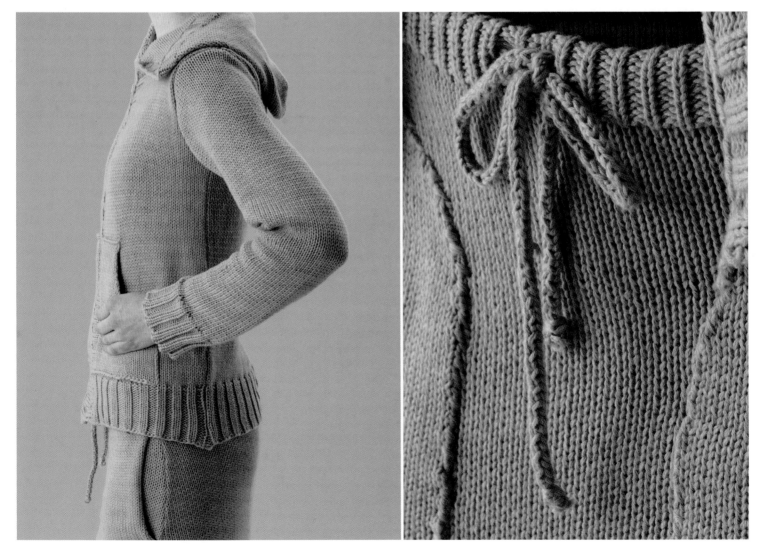

SIZES
SMALL (MEDIUM, LARGE)

FINISHED MEASUREMENTS
HOODIE CHEST: 34" (36", 38")/86.5 (91.5, 96.5) CM
HOODIE LENGTH: 22" (23", 24")/56 (58.5, 61) CM
SKIRT WAIST: 27" (29", 31")/68.5 (73.5, 79) CM
SKIRT LENGTH: 25" (26", 27")/63.5 (66, 68.5) CM

YARN
16 (17, 18) SKEINS SUSS LOVE (100% TACTEL NYLON;
    2 OUNCES/57 GRAMS; 126 YARDS/115 METERS),
    COLOR HEATHER

NOTIONS
1 PAIR SIZE 9 (5.5 MM) CIRCULAR NEEDLES, 24"/61 CM LONG
1 PAIR SIZE 9 (5.5 MM) DOUBLE-POINTED NEEDLES
KNITTING ROW COUNTER (RECOMMENDED)
1 TAPESTRY NEEDLE
1 CREAM-COLORED PLASTIC ZIPPER, 18" (19", 20")/46 (48,
    51) CM IN LENGTH
SEWING NEEDLE AND THREAD IN COMPLEMENTARY COLOR

GAUGE
19 STITCHES AND 24 ROWS = 4"/10 CM IN
    STOCKINETTE STITCH
20 STITCHES AND 24 ROWS = 4"/10 CM IN TWO-BY-TWO
    RIB STITCH

Hoodie

BACK

Cast on 80 (84, 88) stitches. Work in two-by-two rib stitch (knit 2, purl 2, repeat until the end of the row) for 20 rows.

Switch to stockinette stitch (knit all right-side rows and purl all wrong-side rows) until the piece measures 15½" (16½", 17")/39.5 (42, 43) cm from the cast-on edge, ending with a wrong-side row.

ARMHOLE SHAPING

Bind off 4 stitches at the beginning of the next two rows—72 (76, 80) stitches. Decrease 1 stitch at the beginning and end of every other row 4 times—64 (68, 72) stitches. Work even until the piece measures 5½" (5½", 6")/14 (14, 15) cm from the beginning of the armhole shaping, ending with a wrong-side row.

SHOULDER SHAPING

Bind off 8 stitches at the beginning of the next 2 (4, 6) rows—48 (36, 24) stitches. Bind off 6 (6, 0) stitches at the beginning of the next 4 (2, 0) rows—24 stitches remain.

Bind off.

LEFT FRONT

Cast on 40 (44, 44) stitches. Work in a two-by-two rib stitch for 20 rows. Switch to stockinette stitch and work even until the piece measures 15½" (16½", 17")/39.5 (42, 43) cm from the cast-on edge, ending with a wrong-side row.

To shape armhole, bind off 4 stitches at the beginning of the next right-side row—36 (40, 40) stitches. Decrease 1 stitch at the beginning of every right-side row 4 times—32 (36, 36) stitches. Work even until the piece measures 5½" (5½", 6")/14 (14, 15) cm from the beginning of the armhole shaping, ending with a wrong-side row.

To shape shoulders, bind off 8 stitches at the beginning of the next 1 (2, 3) right-side row(s). Bind off 6 (6, 0) stitches at the beginning of the next 2 (1, 0) right-side rows.

At the same time, when the piece measures 18" (19", 20")/46 (48, 51) cm from the cast-on edge, bind off 4 stitches at the beginning of the next wrong-side row. Decrease 2 stitches at the beginning of every wrong-side row 4 (5, 4) times. Work even until the bind-off.

RIGHT FRONT Work as for the Left Front, but reverse shaping.

SLEEVES (Make two) Cast on 40 (40, 44) stitches. Work in two-by-two rib stitch for 20 rows. Switch to stockinette stitch.

Increase 1 stitch at the beginning and end of every 16 (14, 14) rows 7 (9, 9) times—54 (58, 62) stitches. Work even until the piece measures 20" (21", 21½")/51 (53.5, 54.5) cm from the cast-on edge, ending with a wrong-side row.

Bind off 4 stitches at the beginning of the next 2 rows—46 (50, 54) stitches. Decrease 1 stitch at the beginning and end of every 2 rows 9 (8, 5) times—28 (34, 44) stitches. Decrease 1 stitch at the beginning and end of every row 0 (3, 8) times—28 stitches.

Bind off.

LEFT POCKET Cast on 28 stitches. Work even in stockinette stitch for 3"/7.5 cm, or approximately 18 rows, ending with a wrong-side row.

Bind off 5 stitches at the beginning of the next right-side row—23 stitches. Decrease 1 stitch at the beginning of every right-side row and at the end of every wrong-side row for 3 rows—20 stitches. Decrease 1 stitch at the beginning of every right-side row 3 times—17 stitches. Decrease 1 stitch at the beginning of every other right-side row 3 times—14 stitches.

Work even until the Pocket measures 7"/18 cm from the cast-on edge.

Bind off.

RIGHT POCKET Make as for the Left Pocket, but reverse shaping.

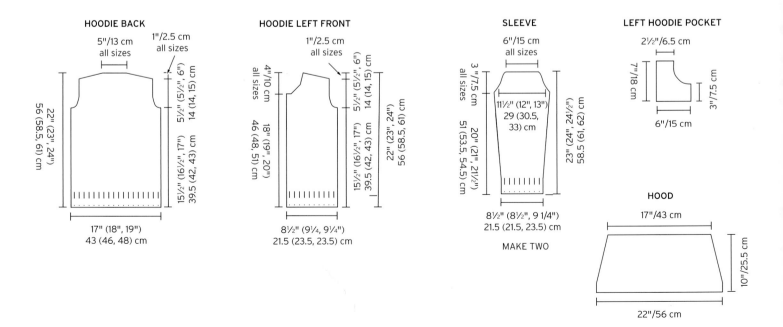

HOODIE BACK
5"/13 cm all sizes
1"/2.5 cm all sizes
5½" (5½", 6") 14 (14, 15) cm
15½" (16½", 17") 39.5 (42, 43) cm
22" (23", 24") 56 (58.5, 61) cm
17" (18", 19") 43 (46, 48) cm

HOODIE LEFT FRONT
1"/2.5 cm all sizes
4"/10 cm all sizes
5½" (5½", 6") 14 (14, 15) cm
18" (19", 20") 46 (48, 51) cm
15½" (16½", 17") 39.5 (42, 43) cm
22" (23", 24") 56 (58.5, 61) cm
8½" (9¼, 9¼") 21.5 (23.5, 23.5) cm

SLEEVE
6"/15 cm all sizes
3"/7.5 cm all sizes
11½" (12", 13") 29 (30.5, 33) cm
20" (21", 21½") 51 (53.5, 54.5) cm
23" (24", 24½") 58.5 (61, 62) cm
8½" (8½", 9 1/4") 21.5 (21.5, 23.5) cm
MAKE TWO

LEFT HOODIE POCKET
2½"/6.5 cm
7"/18 cm
3"/7.5 cm
6"/15 cm

HOOD
17"/43 cm
10"/25.5 cm
22"/56 cm

HOOD

Cast on 104 stitches. Work in two-by-two rib stitch for 8 rows. Switch to stockinette stitch.

Decrease 1 stitch at the beginning and end of every 4 rows 12 times—80 stitches. Work even until the piece measures 10"/25.5 cm from the cast-on edge.

Bind off.

FINISHING

Weave in all loose ends with the tapestry needle.

Pick up 92 (96, 100) stitches along the center edge of the Left Front. Work in two-by-two rib stitch for 8 rows. Bind off loosely in rib pattern. Repeat for the Right Front.

With the tapestry needle and yarn, whipstitch the Pockets into place at the corners formed by the two ribbed edges (see photograph).

Pin shoulder seams and side seams. With the tapestry needle and yarn, backstitch the shoulder and side seams together securely.

Fold Sleeves in half lengthwise with the wrong sides facing out and, with the tapestry needle and yarn, sew together the sleeve seams using backstitch. Pin Sleeves into place at the armholes and, with the tapestry needle and yarn, use backstitch to attach the Sleeves to the armholes.

Pin the Hood into place along the Left Front collar, Back neck, and Right Front collar edges. With the tapestry needle and thread, sew the Hood into place using backstitch.

Pin the zipper into place along the center front edges of the wrong sides of the Left and Right Fronts. With the sewing needle and thread, backstitch the zipper securely to the hoodie.

Skirt

BACK

Cast on 84 (88, 94) stitches. Work in stockinette stitch. Work 1 row even. Cast on 4 stitches at the beginning of every row for 4 rows—100 (104, 110) stitches.

Decrease 1 stitch at the beginning and end of the 10th row from cast-on edge—98 (102, 108) stitches. Decrease 1 stitch at the beginning and end of every 10 (10, 11) rows 9 times—80 (84, 90) stitches. Decrease 1 stitch at the beginning and end of every 6 rows 8 times—64 (68, 74) stitches. Work even until the piece measures 25" (26", 27")/63.5 (66, 68.5) cm from the cast-on edge.

WAISTBAND

Switch to one-by-one rib stitch (knit 1, purl 1, repeat until the end of the row) and work even until the waistband measures 2"/5 cm. Bind off loosely in rib pattern.

FRONT

Work the Front as for the Back until waistband.

WAISTBAND

Work in one-by-one rib stitch for 5 rows.

Work eyelet row as follows: Work 28 (30, 33) stitches, yarn over, work 2 stitches together, work 4 stitches, yarn over, work 2 stitches together, work remaining 28 (30, 33) stitches.

Work in one-by-one rib stitch until waistband measures 2"/5 cm. Bind off loosely in rib pattern.

LEFT POCKET
Cast on 30 stitches. Work even in stockinette stitch until the piece measures 5"/12.5 cm from the cast-on edge, ending with a right-side row. Decrease 1 stitch at the beginning of every other wrong-side row 3 times—27 stitches. Decrease 1 stitch at the beginning of every wrong-side row and the end of every right-side row 13 times—14 stitches.

Bind off.

RIGHT POCKET
Work as for the Left Pocket, but reverse shaping.

TIE
Cast on 4 stitches. Make an I-cord as follows: Knit 4. Switch the needles in your hands; the needle with the stitches is on the left again. With the right side facing you, slide the stitches from the left end of the needle to the right end. Bring the working yarn around the back and knit the 4 stitches. Repeat until you have an I-cord that measures 60"/152.5 cm from the cast-on edge.

Bind off.

FINISHING
Weave in all loose ends with the tapestry needle.

With right sides facing, pin the side seam edges of the Front to the Back. With the tapestry needle and yarn, sew together the side seams using backstitch.

POCKETS
Line up the 9½"/24 cm straight edges of the Pockets with the corresponding side seams and pin into place. With the tapestry needle and yarn, whipstitch the Pockets to the outside of the Front. Along the side seam, whipstitch the top and bottom 2"/5 cm of the straight edge into place, leaving 5½"/14 cm unseamed.

WAISTBAND
To create the waistband casing, fold over the waistband and, with the tapestry needle and yarn, whipstitch the bound-off edge to the inside of the skirt along the line between the skirt body and the one-by-one rib.

Make a knot at both ends of the Tie. Thread the Tie through one of the eyelet holes, around the waistband, and out the other eyelet hole.

LEFT SKIRT POCKET

5"/13 cm

9½"/24 cm

6"/15 cm

SKIRT BACK

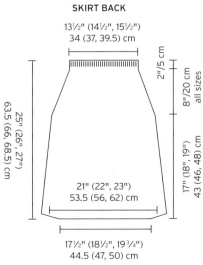

13½" (14½", 15½")
34 (37, 39.5) cm

2"/5 cm

8"/20 cm
all sizes

25" (26", 27")
63.5 (66, 68.5) cm

17" (18", 19")
43 (46, 48) cm

21" (22", 23")
53.5 (56, 62) cm

17½" (18½", 19¾")
44.5 (47, 50) cm

patchwork skirt

EXPERIMENTING WITH LEFTOVER YARN ONE DAY, I CAME UP WITH A PATCHWORK SCARF AND THEN DECIDED TO EXPAND IT INTO A SKIRT. I TRIED TO MATCH YARN WEIGHTS BUT I VARIED THE TEXTURE USING MY SIGNATURE COLORS—RED, GREEN, BROWN, AND CREAM—AND I FINISHED THE SKIRT WITH RED TOPSTITCHING. YOU'LL NEED A SENSE OF ADVEN- TURE TO WEAR THIS PIECE. I LOVE IT WITH A WORN DENIM JACKET AND BOOTS.

SIZES
SMALL (MEDIUM, LARGE, EXTRA-LARGE)

FINISHED MEASUREMENTS
WAIST: 28" (30", 34", 36")/71 (76, 86.5, 91.5) CM
LENGTH: 26" (27", 28", 29")/66 (68.5, 71, 73.5) CM

YARN
A: 2 SKEINS SUSS COTTON (100% COTTON; 2½ OUNCES/
71 GRAMS; 118 YARDS/108 METERS), COLOR LOVE RED
B: 2 SKEINS SUSS ALPACA (100% ALPACA; 2 OUNCES/
57 GRAMS; 163 YARDS/149 METERS), COLOR CAMEL
C: 2 SKEINS SUSS NATURAL SOFT (65% COTTON/35%
RAYON; 2 OUNCES/57 GRAMS; 76 YARDS/69 METERS),
COLOR CREAM
D: 1 SKEIN SUSS BOMULL (100% COTTON; 4 OUNCES/
114 GRAMS; 190 YARDS/174 METERS), COLOR OLIVE
E: 2 SKEINS SUSS ALPACA TWEED (100% ALPACA;
2 OUNCES/57 GRAMS; 148 YARDS/135 METERS),
COLOR CHOCOLATE/NATURAL

NOTIONS
1 PAIR SIZE 8 (5 MM) CIRCULAR NEEDLES, 32"/81 CM LONG
KNITTING ROW COUNTER (RECOMMENDED)
1 SIZE G (4 MM) CROCHET HOOK
1 LARGE TAPESTRY NEEDLE
SEWING NEEDLE AND THREAD IN COMPLEMENTARY COLOR
9"/23 CM INVISIBLE ZIPPER

GAUGE
16 STITCHES AND 20 ROWS = 4"/10 CM IN
STOCKINETTE STITCH
22 STITCHES AND 20 ROWS = 4"/10 CM IN ONE-BY-ONE
RIB STITCH
A NOTE ABOUT GAUGE: IN ORDER TO MAINTAIN CONSISTENT
GAUGE, YOU MAY HAVE TO GO DOWN A NEEDLE SIZE
WHEN WORKING WITH YARN C, SINCE IT HAS SLIGHTLY
MORE TEXTURE THAN THE OTHER YARNS.

NOTE
THROUGHOUT THIS PROJECT, YARN B AND YARN E ARE
WORKED WITH TWO STRANDS HELD TOGETHER.

PANEL A
(Make two)

Cast on 46 (48, 48, 50) stitches with yarn A. Work the following stripe pattern in stockinette stitch (knit all right-side rows and purl all wrong-side rows) while working shaping as indicated:

Work 10 (10, 10, 12) rows with yarn A—10 (10, 10, 12) rows total.

Switch to yarn B and work 20 rows—30 (30, 30, 32) rows total.

Switch to yarn C and work 16 (16, 16, 18) rows—46 (46, 46, 50) rows total.

Switch to yarn D and work 32 (34, 36, 36) rows—78 (80, 82, 86) rows total.

Switch to yarn E and work 10 (10, 12, 12) rows—88 (90, 94, 98) rows total.

Switch to yarn A and work 10 rows—98 (100, 104, 108) rows total.

Switch to yarn B and work 18 (20, 20, 22) rows—116 (120, 124, 130) rows total.

Switch to yarn C and work 14 (16, 16, 16) rows—130 (136, 140, 146) rows total.

At the same time, work shaping as follows: Decrease 1 stitch at the beginning and end of every 10 (10, 12, 12) rows 8 (10, 3, 3) times—30 (28, 42, 44) stitches remain. Decrease 1 stitch at the beginning and end of every 8 (8, 10, 10) rows 6 (4, 10, 10) times—18 (20, 22, 24) stitches remain. Work even until 130 (136, 140, 146) rows total.

Bind off.

PANEL B
(Make two)

Cast on 48 (48, 50, 50) stitches with yarn D. Work the following stripe pattern in stockinette stitch while working shaping as indicated:

Work 32 (36, 36, 36) rows with yarn D—32 (36, 36, 36) rows total.

Switch to yarn E and work 10 (10, 12, 12) rows—42 (46, 48, 48) rows total.

Switch to yarn A and work 10 (10, 10, 12) rows—52 (56, 58, 60) rows total.

Switch to yarn B and work 18 (20, 20, 22) rows—70 (76, 78, 82) rows total.

Switch to yarn C and work 14 (16, 16, 18) rows—84 (92, 94, 100) rows total.

Switch to yarn D and work 36 (34, 36, 36) rows—120 (126, 130, 136) rows total.

Switch to yarn E and work 10 rows—130 (136, 140, 146) rows total.

At the same time, work shaping as follows: Decrease 1 stitch at the beginning and end of every 10 (10, 12, 12) rows 8 (10, 3, 3) times—32 (28, 44, 44) stitches remain. Decrease 1 stitch at the beginning and end of every 8 (8, 10, 10) rows 6 (4, 10, 10) times—20 (20, 24, 24) stitches remain. Work even until 130 (136, 140, 146) rows total.

Bind off.

PANEL C (Make two)

Cast on 46 (48, 48, 50) stitches with yarn C. Work the following stripe pattern in stockinette stitch (knit all right-side rows and purl all wrong-side rows) while working shaping as indicated:

Work 18 (20, 20, 20) rows with yarn C—18 (20, 20, 20) rows total.

Switch to yarn D and work 32 (34, 36, 36) rows—50 (54, 56, 56) rows total.

Switch to yarn E and work 10 (10, 12, 12) rows—60 (64, 68, 68) rows total.

Switch to yarn A and work 10 (10, 10, 12) rows—70 (74, 78, 80) rows total.

Switch to yarn B and work 18 (20, 20, 22) rows—88 (94, 98, 102) rows total.

Switch to yarn C and work 16 (16, 16, 18) rows—104 (110, 114, 120) rows total.

Switch to yarn D and work 26 rows—130 (136, 140, 146) rows total.

At the same time, work shaping as follows: Decrease 1 stitch at the beginning and end of every 10 (10, 12, 12) rows 8 (10, 3, 3) times—30 (28, 42, 44) stitches remain. Decrease 1 stitch at the beginning and end of every 8 (8, 10, 10) rows 6 (4, 10, 10) times—18 (20, 22, 24) stitches remain. Work even until 130 (136, 140, 146) rows total.

Bind off.

FINISHING

Weave in any loose ends with the tapestry needle.

With the crochet hook and yarn A, use slipstitch to join the Panels together in the order indicated by the diagram (page 78). To form a skirt shape, slipstitch the right edge of C2 to the left edge of A1. In order to attach the zipper, leave 7"/18 cm unjoined at the top of the skirt.

With the crochet hook and yarn A, work a single crochet stitch around the bottom hem of the skirt.

WAISTBAND

Starting at the zipper opening, pick up 112 (120, 136, 144) stitches around the waistband of the skirt with yarn A. Work in a one-by-one rib stitch pattern (knit 1, purl 1, repeat until the end of the row) until waistband measures 2"/5 cm. Bind off *loosely* in rib pattern.

Pin zipper in place. With sewing needle and thread, whipstitch zipper to opening in the side seam and waistband.

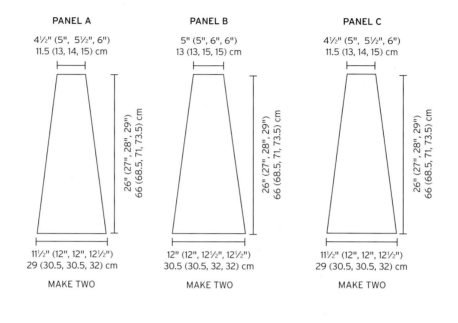

PANEL A

4½" (5", 5½", 6")
11.5 (13, 14, 15) cm

26" (27", 28", 29")
66 (68.5, 71, 73.5) cm

11½" (12", 12", 12½")
29 (30.5, 30.5, 32) cm

MAKE TWO

PANEL B

5" (5", 6", 6")
13 (13, 15, 15) cm

26" (27", 28", 29")
66 (68.5, 71, 73.5) cm

12" (12", 12½", 12½")
30.5 (30.5, 32, 32) cm

MAKE TWO

PANEL C

4½" (5", 5½", 6")
11.5 (13, 14, 15) cm

26" (27", 28", 29")
66 (68.5, 71, 73.5) cm

11½" (12", 12", 12½")
29 (30.5, 30.5, 32) cm

MAKE TWO

ASSEMBLY DIAGRAM

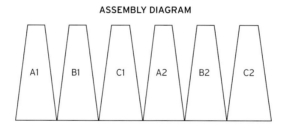

A1 B1 C1 A2 B2 C2

dresses

off-the-shoulder dress

I WAS WATCHING AN OLD AUDREY HEPBURN MOVIE WHEN I DREAMED UP THIS DRESS. CAN'T YOU JUST PICTURE HER IN IT? YOU KNIT IT IN BURGUNDY AND PINK. I THINK IT'S FEMININE AND SOFT ENOUGH TO WEAR WITH HIGH HEELS FOR A GLAMOROUS EVENING ON THE TOWN. OR WEAR IT WITH BOOTS FOR A DAY AT THE OFFICE.

4

5

SIZES
SMALL (MEDIUM, LARGE)

FINISHED MEASUREMENTS
CHEST: 32" (34", 36")/81 (86.5, 91.5) CM
LENGTH: 37" (38", 39")/94 (96.5, 99) CM (NOT
INCLUDING COLLAR)

YARNS
A: 11 (12, 13) SKEINS SUSS COTTON (100% COTTON;
2.5 OUNCES/71 GRAMS; 118 YARDS/108 METERS), COLOR
BROWNSTONE
B: 2 SKEINS SUSS FUZZY (60% COTTON/40% POLYAMIDE;
2 OUNCES/57 GRAMS; 67 YARDS/61 METERS), COLOR
BURGUNDY ROSE

NOTIONS
1 PAIR SIZE 13 (9 MM) CIRCULAR NEEDLES, 24"/61 CM LONG
1 PAIR SIZE 11 (8 MM) CIRCULAR NEEDLES, 24"/61 CM LONG
KNITTING ROW COUNTER (RECOMMENDED)
2 STITCH HOLDERS
1 LARGE TAPESTRY NEEDLE

GAUGE
10 STITCHES AND 13 ROWS = 4"/10 CM IN STOCKINETTE
STITCH WITH TWO STRANDS YARN A HELD TOGETHER
12 STITCHES AND 14 ROWS = 4"/10 CM IN TWO-BY-TWO RIB
STITCH WITH TWO STRANDS YARN B HELD TOGETHER

BACK

Cast on 56 (58, 60) stitches with two strands of yarn A held together on larger needles. Work in stockinette stitch (knit all right-side rows and purl all wrong-side rows). Work 1 row even.

Cast on 2 stitches at the beginning of the next 4 rows—64 (66, 68) stitches. Decrease 1 stitch at the beginning and end of every 6 rows 12 times—40 (42, 44) stitches. Work even until the piece measures 32" (32½", 33")/81 (82.5, 84) cm from the cast-on edge, ending with a wrong-side row.

**ARMHOLE
SHAPING**

Bind off 2 stitches at the beginning of the next 2 rows—36 (38, 40) stitches. Decrease 1 stitch at the beginning and end of the next 8 (9, 10) wrong-side rows—20 stitches remain. Work one row even.

Place remaining stitches on stitch holder.

FRONT

Work the Front as for the Back.

**SLEEVES
(Make two)**

Cast on 20 (24, 24) stitches with two strands of yarn B held together on the smaller needles. Work in two-by-two rib stitch (knit 2, purl 2, repeat until the end of the row) for 10 rows.

Switch to larger needles. Work in stockinette stitch with two strands of yarn A held together. Increase 1 stitch at the beginning and end of every 4 (5, 4) rows 5 (4, 5) times—30 (32, 34) stitches.

To shape sleeve caps, bind off 2 stitches at the beginning of the next 2 rows—26 (28, 30) stitches. Decrease 1 stitch at the beginning and end of the next 8 (9, 10) wrong-side rows—10 stitches remain. Work one row even.

Bind off.

FINISHING   Weave in all loose ends with the tapestry needle.

Fold Sleeves in half lengthwise with right sides facing and pin seams. With the tapestry needle and one strand of yarn A, sew together the sleeve seams using backstitch.

Place the Front and Back pieces together with the right sides facing each other and pin together the side seams. With the tapestry needle and one strand of yarn A, sew together the side seams using backstitch.

Pin Sleeves into armhole/neckline shaping. With the tapestry needle and one strand of yarn A, sew the Sleeves into place using backstitch.

COLLAR   With the smaller needles and two strands of yarn B held together, pick up 20 stitches from stitch holder on Back, 12 stitches from right Sleeve bind-off edge, 20 stitches from stitch holder on Front, and 12 stitches from left Sleeve bind-off edge—64 stitches total. Join for working in the round. Work in two-by-two rib stitch for 12 rows. Bind off *loosely* in rib pattern.

BACK/FRONT

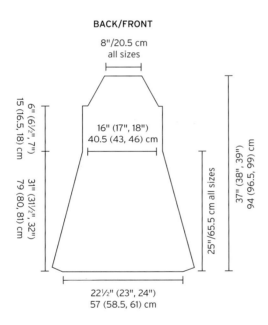

8"/20.5 cm
all sizes

6" (6½", 7")
15 (16.5, 18) cm

16" (17", 18")
40.5 (43, 46) cm

37" (38", 39")
94 (96.5, 99) cm

25"/65.5 cm all sizes

31" (31½", 32")
79 (80, 81) cm

22½" (23", 24")
57 (58.5, 61) cm

SLEEVE

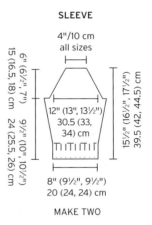

4"/10 cm
all sizes

6" (6½", 7")
15 (16.5, 18) cm

9½" (10", 10½")
24 (25.5, 26) cm

12" (13", 13½")
30.5 (33, 34) cm

15½" (16½", 17½")
39.5 (42, 44.5) cm

8" (9½", 9½")
20 (24, 24) cm

MAKE TWO

embroidered dress

THIS DRESS, WITH ITS EASY-TO-WEAR, SLIGHT A-LINE, WAS A GREAT HIT ON THE RUNWAY. ALTHOUGH IT'S NOT VERY FITTED, IT GIVES THE ILLUSION OF SKIMMING THE BODY. I KEPT THE SHAPE SIMPLE BECAUSE THE EMBROIDERY IS SO DETAILED. AFTER YOU'VE KNIT IN A TEXTURED YARN, IT'S FUN TO ADD ANOTHER TEXTURE WITH EMBROIDERY. THE LITTLE SUMMER FLOWERS ARE FROM AN OLD SWEDISH BOOK.

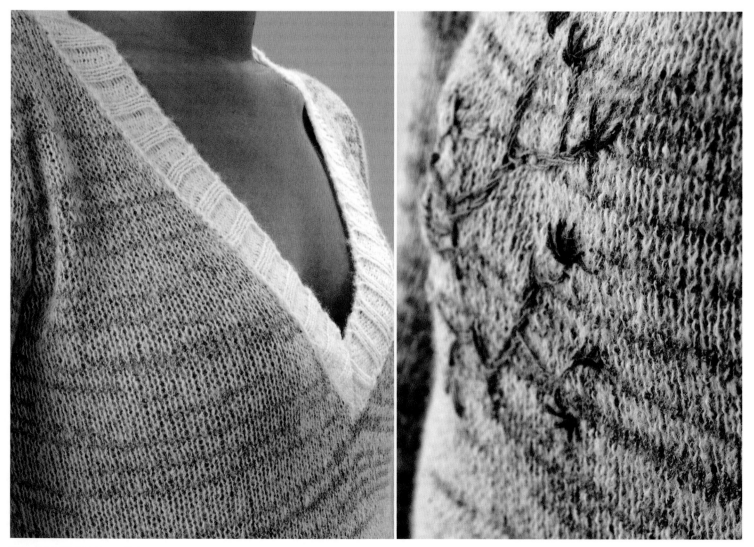

3

SIZES
SMALL (MEDIUM, LARGE)

FINISHED MEASUREMENTS
CHEST: 32" (34", 36")/81 (86.5, 91.5) CM
LENGTH: 50" (52", 52½")/127 (132, 133.5) CM

YARN
A: 13 (13, 14) SKEINS SUSS ULTRASOFT (40% VISCOSE/
30% ALPACA/20% ACRYLIC/10% NYLON; 1½ OUNCES/
43 GRAMS; 204 YARDS/187 METERS), COLOR SEAWEED
B: 1 SKEIN SUSS FISHNET (53% ACRYLIC/30% NYLON/
17% ALPACA; 1½ OUNCES/43 GRAMS; 285 YARDS/
261 METERS), COLOR IVORY
C: 1 BALL SUSS PERLE COTTON (100% COTTON; 2 OUNCES/
57 GRAMS; 256 YARDS/234 METERS), COLOR WILLOW
D: 1 BALL SUSS PERLE COTTON (100% COTTON; 2 OUNCES/
57 GRAMS; 256 YARDS/234 METERS), COLOR PINK
CORAL

E: 1 BALL SUSS PERLE COTTON (100% COTTON; 2 OUNCES/
57 GRAMS; 256 YARDS/234 METERS), COLOR
PERSIMMON

NOTIONS
1 PAIR SIZE 4 (3.5 MM) CIRCULAR NEEDLES, 32"/81 CM LONG
KNITTING ROW COUNTER (RECOMMENDED)
1 TAPESTRY NEEDLE
SEWING PINS
SEWING NEEDLE AND THREAD IN COMPLEMENTARY COLORS
TRACING PAPER
STITCH HOLDER

GAUGE
24 STITCHES AND 30 ROWS = 4"/10CM IN STOCKINETTE
STITCH WITH YARN A
26 STITCHES AND 32 ROWS = 4"/10 CM IN TWO-BY-TWO RIB
STITCH WITH YARN B

BACK

Cast on 168 (174, 180) stitches with yarn A. Work in stockinette stitch (knit all right-side rows and purl all wrong-side rows). Work 1 row even.

Cast on 6 stitches at the beginning of the next 8 rows—216 (222, 228) stitches total.

Decrease 1 stitch at the beginning and end of every 4 rows 67 times—82 (88, 94) stitches total. Work even until the piece measures 37½"/95 cm from the cast-on edge, ending with a wrong-side row.

Increase 1 stitch at the beginning and end of every 10 rows 3 (4, 4) times—88 (96, 102) stitches total. Work even until the piece measures 43½" (45", 45")/110.5 (114.5, 114.5) cm.

ARMHOLE SHAPING

Bind off 6 stitches at the beginning of the next 2 rows—76 (84, 90) stitches total. Decrease 1 stitch at the beginning and end of every wrong-side row 6 times—64 (72, 78) stitches total. Work even until the piece measures 6" (6½", 7")/15 (16.5, 18) cm from the beginning of armhole shaping.

SHOULDER SHAPING

Bind off 4 (5, 7) stitches at the beginning of the next 4 (4, 2) rows—48 (52, 64) stitches total. Bind off 0 (0, 6) stitches at the beginning of the next 0 (0, 2) rows.

Bind off remaining 48 (52, 52) stitches.

FRONT

Work as for the Back until the piece measures 38" (40", 40½")/96.5 (101.5, 103) cm, ending with a wrong-side row.

Work half the stitches on the needle and place the remaining stitches on a stitch holder.

LEFT FRONT

Work from needle. Decrease 1 stitch every 3 rows on collar edge 12 (16, 16) times. Decrease 1 stitch every 4 rows on collar edge 12 (10, 10) times.

At the same time, work even on side seam edge until the piece measures 43½" (45", 45")/110.5 (114.5, 114.5) cm. Bind off 6 stitches at the beginning of the next right-side row. Decrease 1 stitch at the end of every wrong-side row 6 times. Work even until the piece measures 6" (6½", 7")/15 (16.5, 18) cm from the beginning of armhole shaping. Bind off 4 (5, 7) stitches at the beginning of the next 2 (2, 1) right-side rows. Bind off 0 (0, 6) stitches at the beginning of the next 0 (0, 1) right-side row.

RIGHT FRONT

Pick up stitches on the stitch holder and work the right front as for the left front, but reverse shaping.

SLEEVES (Make two)

Cast on 51 (54, 56) stitches with yarn A. Work in stockinette stitch.

Increase 1 stitch at the beginning and end of every 16 (16, 15) rows 9 (10, 11) times—69 (74, 78) stitches. Work even until the sleeve measures 21" (22", 22½")/53.5 (56, 57) cm, ending with a wrong-side row.

Bind off 6 stitches at the beginning of the next 2 rows—57 (62, 66) stitches. Decrease 1 stitch at the beginning and end of every wrong-side row 8 times—41 (46, 50) stitches. Decrease 1 stitch at the beginning and end of every row 6 times—29 (34, 38) stitches.

Bind off.

FINISHING

Weave in all loose ends with the tapestry needle.

Place the Back and Front pieces together with the right sides facing each other. Pin shoulder and side seams together. With the sewing needle and thread, sew the shoulder and side seams together using backstitch. To maintain the light feel of this garment, join seams with a very small seam allowance. You can also use a sewing machine to finish this dress.

Fold Sleeves in half lengthwise with the right sides facing each other and pin together. With the sewing needle and thread, sew together the sleeve seams using backstitch.

With the sewing needle and thread, sew the Sleeves into the armholes using backstitch. You may find it helpful to turn the piece inside out and pin the Sleeves into the armhole first. Make sure you pin the Sleeves evenly so there is no bunching or stretching.

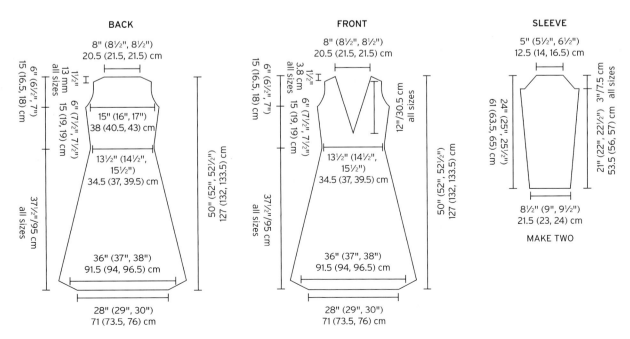

COLLAR   Start at the bottom of the "V" neckline, and pick up 90 stitches along the left Front collar edge, 48 (52, 52) stitches along Back neck edge, and 90 stitches along the right Front collar edge—228 (232, 232) stitches total. Work in two-by-two rib stitch (knit 2, purl 2, repeat until the end of the row) until the collar measures 1½"/3.8 cm. Bind off loosely in rib pattern.

Fold over the ends of the ribbed collar at the bottom center of the "V" neckline toward the wrong side of the piece. Fold the corners at a 45-degree angle to form a vertical line where the two edges meet at the bottom of the "V." With the sewing needle and thread, whipstitch this seam together securely. With the sewing needle and thread, tack down the edges of the collar on the wrong side of the sweater along the line of picked-up stitches.

EMBROIDERY   Copy the floral embroidery patterns provided onto several pieces of tracing paper. Pin the pieces of paper to the Front piece. Pattern A should begin just below the waist on the right side. Pattern B should be placed in the right hip area, and Pattern C should be placed just below and to the right. See photograph for placement suggestion.

With the tapestry needle and two strands of yarn C, embroider the vines and stems first. Use chain stitch for the vines and straight stitch for the stems (see photograph). With the tapestry needle, make straight stitch flowers, using either two strands of yarn D or two strands of yarn E, as indicated on charts. When you are done embroidering, simply tear away the tracing paper. Any leftover scraps can be removed with tweezers.

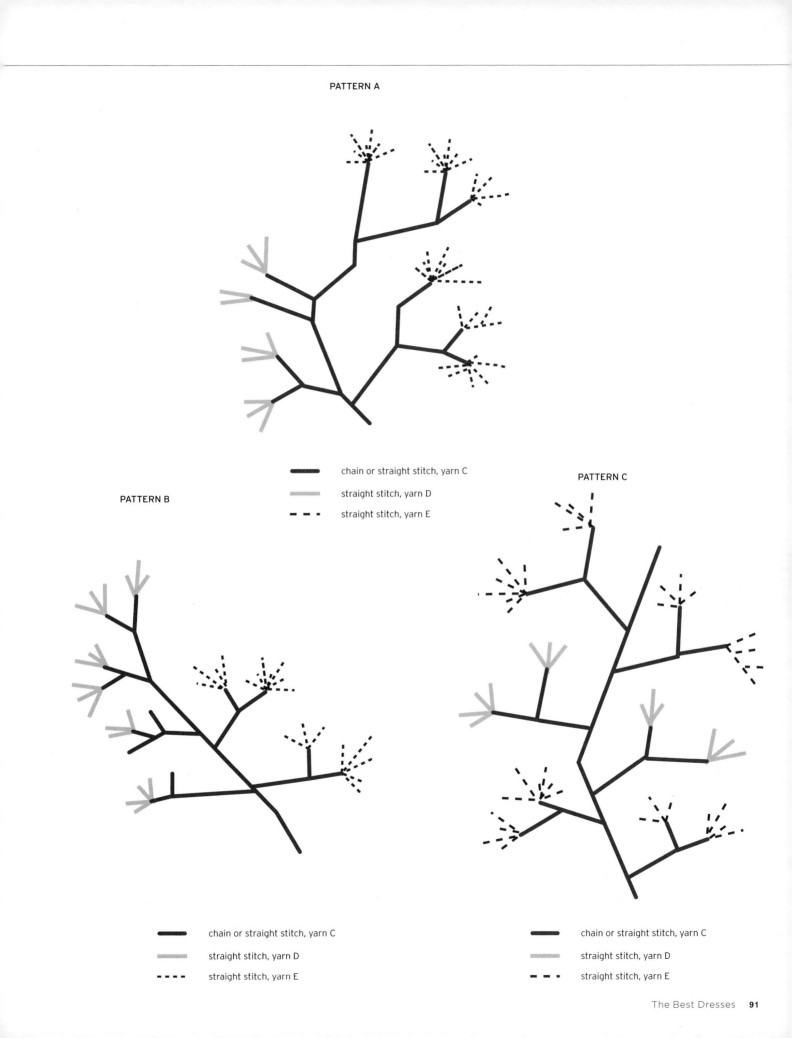

PATTERN A

PATTERN B

PATTERN C

—— chain or straight stitch, yarn C

—— straight stitch, yarn D

- - - straight stitch, yarn E

—— chain or straight stitch, yarn C

—— straight stitch, yarn D

- - - straight stitch, yarn E

—— chain or straight stitch, yarn C

—— straight stitch, yarn D

- - - straight stitch, yarn E

shirtdress

IN THIS PATTERN, I HAVE TAKEN A CONSERVATIVE, CLASSIC DESIGN—THE SHIRTDRESS—AND GIVEN IT A HIGH-FASHION TWIST. SPARKLING BRIGHT IN WHITE SNUGGLE YARN, THIS DESIGN FEATURES SLEEVES WITH A DEEP RIB AT THE CUFFS AND TINY LITTLE SNAPS THAT YOU LEAVE OPEN. YOU CAN WEAR IT AS A DRESS, BUT IT ALSO LOOKS COOL WORN AS A TUNIC OVER PANTS.

SIZE
SMALL (MEDIUM, LARGE)

FINISHED MEASUREMENTS
CHEST: 34" (36", 38")/86.5 (91.5, 96.5) CM
LENGTH (INCLUDING COLLAR): 37" (38", 39")/
  94 (96.5, 99) CM

YARN
15 (15, 16) SKEINS SUSS SNUGGLE (60% COTTON/40%
  ACRYLIC; 2 OUNCES/57 GRAMS; 126 YARDS/115 METERS),
  COLOR WHITE

NOTIONS
1 PAIR SIZE 8 (5 MM) CIRCULAR NEEDLES, 24"/61 CM LONG
1 KNITTING ROW COUNTER (RECOMMENDED)
STITCH MARKER (OPTIONAL)
1 LARGE TAPESTRY NEEDLE
SEWING PINS
1 PACKAGE METAL SNAP TAPE, WHITE, ¾"/2 CM WIDE, 1½"/
  3.8 CM SPACING (AVAILABLE AT MOST FABRIC STORES)
SEWING NEEDLE AND WHITE THREAD
2 ROCK/SHELL BUTTONS, ½"/13 MM IN DIAMETER
  (AVAILABLE AT WWW.SUSSDESIGN.COM)
1 SIZE H (5 MM) CROCHET HOOK

GAUGE
18 STITCHES AND 24 ROWS = 4"/10 CM IN
  STOCKINETTE STITCH
26 STITCHES AND 24 ROWS = 4"/10 CM IN TWO-BY-TWO
  RIB STITCH

BACK

Cast on 86 (90, 94) stitches. Work in stockinette stitch (knit all right-side rows and purl all wrong-side rows). Work 1 row even. Cast on 5 stitches at the beginning of the next 6 rows—116 (120, 124) stitches total.

Decrease 1 stitch at the beginning and end of every 5 (6, 6) rows 22 (14, 14) times—72 (92, 96) stitches. Decrease 1 stitch at the beginning and end of every 0 (5, 5) rows 0 (8, 8) times—72 (76, 80) stitches. Work even until the piece measures 21" (22", 22")/53.5 (56, 56) cm, ending with a wrong-side row.

Increase 1 stitch at the beginning and end of every 20 (16, 16) rows 2 (3, 3) times—76 (82, 86) stitches. Work even until the piece measures 29½" (30½", 31")/75 (77.5, 79) cm from the cast-on edge, ending with a wrong-side row.

Bind off 4 stitches at the beginning of the next 2 rows—68 (74, 78) stitches. Decrease 1 stitch at the beginning and end of every other row 3 times—62 (68, 72) stitches. Work even until the piece measures 36" (37", 38")/91.5 (94, 96.5) cm, ending with a wrong-side row.

Bind off 5 (6, 6) stitches at the beginning of the next 2 (2, 6) rows—52 (56, 36) stitches. Bind off 4 (5, 0) stitches at the beginning of the next 4 (4, 0) rows—36 stitches.

Bind off.

LEFT FRONT

Cast on 48 (50, 52) stitches. Work in stockinette stitch. Work 1 row even. Cast on 5 stitches at the beginning of the next 3 right-side rows—63 (65, 67) stitches.

The Front pieces are worked with different shaping on each side. Make sure you follow both sets of instructions at the same time.

On the side seam edge (the right edge when the right side is facing you), decrease 1 stitch every 5 (6, 6) rows 22 (14, 14) times—41 (51, 53) stitches. Decrease 1 stitch every 0 (5, 5) rows 0 (8, 8) times—41 (43, 45) stitches. Work even until the piece measures 21" (22", 22")/53.5 (56, 56) cm, ending with a wrong-side row.

Increase 1 stitch every 20 (16, 16) rows 2 (3, 3) times. Work even until the piece measures 29½" (30½", 31")/75 (77.5, 79) cm from cast-on edge, ending with a wrong-side row.

To shape armholes, bind off 4 stitches at the beginning of the next row. Decrease 1 stitch every other row 3 times. Work even until the piece measures 36" (37", 38")/91.5 (94, 96.5) cm, ending with a wrong-side row. To shape shoulders, bind off 5 (6, 6) stitches at the beginning of the next 1 (1, 3) row(s). Bind off 4 (5, 0) stitches at the beginning of the next 2 (2, 0) rows.

On the center front edge (the left edge when the right side is facing you), work even until the piece measures 27" (28", 29")/68.5 (71, 73.5) cm from the cast-on edge, ending with a right-side row. Place a stitch marker or tie a contrasting piece of yarn at this row. Decrease 1 stitch every 5 rows 7 times. Bind off 3 stitches at the beginning of the row 6"/15 cm from stitch marker. Decrease 1 stitch every row 8 times. Decrease 1 stitch every other row 5 times. Work even until shoulder seam bind off.

RIGHT FRONT

Work as for the Left Front, but reverse shaping.

**SLEEVES
(Make two)**

Cast on 40 (40, 44) stitches. Work in two-by-two rib stitch (knit 2, purl 2, repeat until the end of the row) for 18 rows.

Switch to stockinette stitch. Increase 1 stitch at the beginning and end of every 15 (14, 14) rows 6 (7, 7) times—52 (54, 58) stitches. Work even until the sleeve measures 19" (20", 20½")/48 (51, 52) cm from the cast-on edge, ending with a wrong-side row.

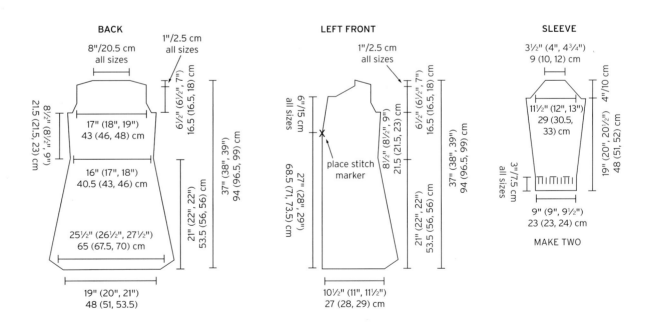

BACK

8"/20.5 cm
all sizes

1"/2.5 cm
all sizes

6½" (6½", 7")
16.5 (16.5, 18) cm

17" (18", 19")
43 (46, 48) cm

8½" (8½", 9")
21.5 (215, 23) cm

16" (17", 18")
40.5 (43, 46) cm

37" (38", 39")
94 (96.5, 99) cm

21" (22", 22")
53.5 (56, 56) cm

25½" (26½", 27½")
65 (67.5, 70) cm

19" (20", 21")
48 (51, 53.5)

LEFT FRONT

1"/2.5 cm
all sizes

6"/15 cm
all sizes

6½" (6½", 7")
16.5 (16.5, 18) cm

8½" (8½", 9")
21.5 (21.5, 23) cm

place stitch
marker

27" (28", 29")
68.5 (71, 73.5) cm

37" (38", 39")
94 (96.5, 99) cm

21" (22", 22")
53.5 (56, 56) cm

10½" (11", 11½")
27 (28, 29) cm

SLEEVE

3½" (4", 4¾")
9 (10, 12) cm

4"/10 cm

11½" (12", 13")
29 (30.5, 33) cm

19" (20", 20½")
48 (51, 52) cm

3"/7.5 cm
all sizes

9" (9", 9½")
23 (23, 24) cm

MAKE TWO

Bind off 4 stitches at the beginning of the next 2 rows—44 (46, 50) stitches. Decrease 1 stitch at the beginning and end of every other row 10 times—24 (26, 30) stitches. Decrease 1 stitch at the beginning and end of every row 4 times—16 (18, 22) stitches.

Bind off.

COLLAR

Cast on 76 stitches. Work in stockinette stitch.

Decrease 1 stitch at the beginning and end of every 4 rows 4 times—60 stitches. Bind off 3 stitches at the beginning of the next 8 rows—36 stitches. Bind off all stitches.

**POCKET COVERS
(Make two)**

Cast on 17 stitches. Work even in stockinette stitch for 8 rows. Work an eyelet row as follows: Work 8 stitches, yarn over, work 2 stitches together, work remaining 7 stitches. Work 2 rows even.

Decrease 1 stitch at the beginning and end of every wrong-side row 8 times.

Bind off remaining stitch.

BELT

Cast on 12 stitches. Work in two-by-two rib stitch until belt measures 60"/152.5 cm, or desired length.

Bind off in rib pattern.

FINISHING

Weave in all loose ends with the tapestry needle.

Pin together the shoulder and side seams. With the tapestry needle and yarn, sew together the shoulder and side seams using backstitch.

Fold Sleeves lengthwise with the right sides facing each other and, with the tapestry needle and yarn, sew together the sleeve seams using backstitch. Leave the last 12"/30.5 cm at the cuff unseamed. With the sewing needle and thread, whipstitch 6½"/16.5 cm of snap tape to the inside of the cuff opening at the wrist. Make sure the stitches do not show on the outside of the Sleeve.

With the tapestry needle and yarn, sew the Sleeves into the armholes using backstitch. You may find it helpful to turn the piece inside out and pin the Sleeves into the armholes first. Make sure you pin the Sleeves evenly so there is no bunching or stretching.

With the sewing needle and thread, start at the stitch marker and whipstitch 20"/51 cm of snap tape to the inside lapel of the Left and Right Fronts. Make sure the stitches do not show on the outside of the garment.

Starting at the center of the Back neck, pin the Collar into place so the right side will be showing when the garment is worn. With the crochet hook and yarn, work a single crochet stitch join on the *outside* of the jacket to attach the Collar.

POCKET COVERS

With the sewing needle and thread, backstitch the top edge of one of the Pocket Covers to the Left Front approximately 3"/7.5 cm below the bottom edge of the collar and 1½"/3.8 cm from the center front edge. Repeat for the second Pocket Cover and the Right Front.

With the sewing needle and thread, attach one button to the Left Front and one to the Right Front where indicated by the pocket placement.

BELT LOOPS With the crochet hook and two strands of yarn held together, make two chains approximately 4"/10 cm long. With the tapestry needle and yarn, attach these chain loops securely to the side seams so the top of the loop lies approximately 8"/20.5 cm below the bottom of the armhole. Try on the garment and mark where you think the Belt should be placed.

When you're done with the belt loops, thread the Belt through the two loops.

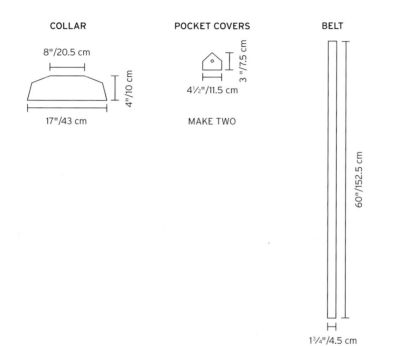

COLLAR

8"/20.5 cm

4"/10 cm

17"/43 cm

POCKET COVERS

3"/7.5 cm

4½"/11.5 cm

MAKE TWO

BELT

60"/152.5 cm

1¾"/4.5 cm

sleeveless turtleneck dress

THIS DRESS WAS INSPIRED BY A VINTAGE CARDIGAN THAT I FELL IN LOVE WITH WHILE BROWSING THROUGH A *VOGUE KNITTING* MAGAZINE FROM THE FORTIES. IT FALLS FROM THE RIBBED TURTLENECK IN AN A-LINE TO ABOVE THE KNEE, AND YOU CAN WEAR IT WITH OR WITHOUT THE BELT. KNIT IN SOFT AQUA AND DARK TAUPE ANGORA, THE DRESS IS LIGHT ENOUGH FOR EVERY SEASON EXCEPT SUMMER. IN THE WINTER, IT LAYERS WELL OVER A LONG-SLEEVE T-SHIRT.

SIZE
SMALL (MEDIUM, LARGE)

FINISHED MEASUREMENTS
CHEST: 34" (36", 38")/86.5 (91.5, 96.5) CM
LENGTH (INCLUDING COLLAR): 43½" (44½", 45½")/
    110.5 (113, 115.5) CM

YARN
A: 7 SKEINS SUSS ANGORA (70% ANGORA/30% NYLON;
    1½ OUNCES/43 GRAMS; 246 YARDS/225 METERS),
    COLOR TAUPE
B: 7 SKEINS SUSS ANGORA (70% ANGORA/30% NYLON;
    1½ OUNCES/43 GRAMS; 246 YARDS/225 METERS),
    COLOR AQUA

NOTIONS
1 PAIR SIZE 9 (5.5 MM) CIRCULAR NEEDLES, 24"/61 CM LONG
1 PAIR SIZE 8 (5 MM) CIRCULAR NEEDLES, 16"/40.5 CM LONG
1 KNITTING ROW COUNTER
1 LARGE STITCH HOLDER
1 LARGE TAPESTRY NEEDLE

SEWING PINS
1 SIZE G (4 MM) CROCHET HOOK

GAUGE
16 STITCHES AND 20 ROWS = 4"/10 CM IN STOCKINETTE
    STITCH WITH LARGER NEEDLES AND FOUR STRANDS OF
    YARN HELD TOGETHER
22 STITCHES AND 20 ROWS = 4"/10 CM IN ONE-BY-ONE RIB
    STITCH WITH LARGER NEEDLES AND FOUR STRANDS OF
    YARN HELD TOGETHER
24 STITCHES AND 22 ROWS = 4"/10 CM IN ONE-BY-ONE RIB
    STITCH WITH SMALLER NEEDLES AND FOUR STRANDS
    OF YARN HELD TOGETHER
A NOTE ABOUT GAUGE: SINCE THIS GARMENT IS WORKED
    THROUGHOUT WITH TWO STRANDS OF YARN A AND
    TWO STRANDS OF YARN B HELD TOGETHER, GAUGE WAS
    CALCULATED FOR THIS AMOUNT. YOU MAY FIND IT
    HELPFUL TO WIND THE SKEINS INTO BALLS CONSISTING
    OF TWO STRANDS OF YARN A OR TWO STRANDS OF
    YARN B BEFORE BEGINNING TO KNIT. PULL YARN FROM
    BOTH BALLS AS YOU WORK.

BACK

Using the larger needles, cast on 60 (64, 68) stitches with two strands of yarn A and two strands of yarn B held together. Purl 1 row (wrong-side row). Work in stockinette stitch (knit all right-side rows and purl all wrong-side rows). Cast on 4 stitches at the beginning of every row for 6 rows—84 (88, 92) stitches total.

Decrease 1 stitch at the beginning and end of every 16 (17, 17) rows 8 times—68 (72, 76) stitches. Work even until the piece measures 28½" (29", 29½")/72.5 (73.5, 75) cm, or approximately 142 (144, 146) rows, ending with a wrong-side row.

ARMHOLE SHAPING

Bind off 4 stitches at the beginning of the next 2 rows—60 (64, 68) stitches. Decrease 1 stitch at the beginning and end of every other row 6 times—48 (52, 56) stitches. Work even until the piece measures 34" (35", 36")/86.5 (89, 91.5) cm.

SHOULDER SHAPING

Bind off 3 (4, 4) stitches at the beginning of the next 4 rows—36 (36, 40) stitches.

TURTLENECK

Work in one-by-one rib stitch (knit 1, purl 1, repeat until the end of the row) until turtleneck measures 8½"/21.5 cm from the shoulder seam. Bind off *loosely* to ensure sufficient room to pull the dress over your head.

FRONT

Work as for the Back until the piece measures 33" (34", 35")/84 (86.5, 89) cm, ending with a wrong-side row.

Next row: Work 14 (16, 16) stitches and place remaining 34 (36, 40) stitches on stitch holder.

LEFT NECKLINE

Work from needle. Bind off 2 stitches at the beginning of the next 4 wrong-side rows. *At the same time,* work even on armhole edge for 4 rows. Bind off 3 (4, 4) stitches at the beginning of the next 2 right-side rows.

RIGHT NECKLINE Starting at the armhole edge, pick up and knit 14 (16, 16) stitches from the stitch holder. Leave remaining 20 (20, 24) middle stitches on the stitch holder. Work from needle as for the left neckline, but reverse shaping.

TURTLENECK Pick up 10 stitches along right neckline edge, pick up 20 (20, 24) stitches from stitch holder, and pick up 10 stitches from left neckline edge—40 (40, 44) stitches total.

Work in a one-by-one rib stitch until turtleneck measures 8½"/21.5 cm from the shoulder seam. Bind off *loosely* to ensure sufficient room to pull the dress over your head.

BELT Cast on 12 stitches with the smaller needles. Work in one-by-one rib stitch until the belt measures 60"/152.5 cm (approximately 330 rows), or desired length.

Bind off in rib pattern.

FINISHING Weave in all loose ends with the tapestry needle.

Pin together the shoulder and collar seams. With the tapestry needle and two strands of yarn A and two strands of yarn B, sew together the shoulder and collar seams using backstitch. Pin the side seams together and sew the side seams using backstitch.

With the smaller needles, start at the bottom of the armhole and pick up 76 (80, 84) stitches along the armhole edge. Work in one-by-one rib stitch in the round for 8 rows. Bind off loosely. Repeat for the other armhole.

With the crochet hook and two strands of yarn A and two strands of yarn B, work a single crochet around the entire bottom hem of the dress.

BELT LOOPS With the crochet hook and two strands of yarn A and two strands of yarn B, make two chains approximately 3"/7.5 cm long. With the tapestry needle and two strands of yarn A and two strands of yarn B, attach these chain loops securely to the side seams so that the top of the loop lies approximately 4"/10 cm below the bottom of the armhole. You may want to try on the garment first and mark where you think the Belt should be placed.

Thread the Belt through the belt loops.

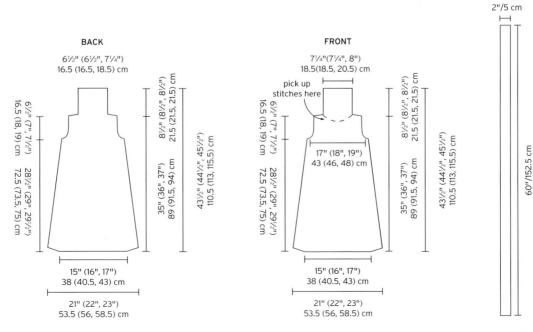

coats & capes

zigzag coat

WHEN I WAS THIRTEEN, I WORE A CREAM-COLORED COAT LIKE THIS, WITH SPECIAL REINDEER HORN BUTTONS. I ADDED ZIGZAG CABLES ON THE SLEEVES AND USED ARAN-COLORED WOOL YARN FOR THIS WOMAN'S VERSION. A HOOD IS THE TRADITIONAL PROTECTION AGAINST SWEDISH WINTERS, BUT THIS ONE HAS A CLEANER, MORE CONTEMPORARY CUT.

SIZES
SMALL (MEDIUM, LARGE)

FINISHED MEASUREMENTS
CHEST: 38" (40", 42")/96.5 (101.5, 106.5) CM
LENGTH: 35" (36", 37")/ 89 (91.5, 94) CM

YARN
23 (23, 24) SKEINS SUSS ULL (100% WOOL; 2 OUNCES/
57 GRAMS; 215 YARDS/197 METERS), COLOR ARAN

NOTIONS
1 PAIR SIZE 10 (6 MM) CIRCULAR NEEDLES, 24"/61 CM LONG
1 PAIR SIZE 9 (5.5 MM) NEEDLES
1 CABLE NEEDLE
1 KNITTING ROW COUNTER (RECOMMENDED)
1 LARGE TAPESTRY NEEDLE
SEWING PINS
1 SIZE G (4 MM) CROCHET HOOK

3 WOODEN HORN BUTTONS
SEWING NEEDLE AND THREAD IN COMPLEMENTARY COLOR

GAUGE
16 STITCHES AND 20 ROWS = 4"/10 CM IN STOCKINETTE
STITCH WITH TWO STRANDS HELD TOGETHER ON
LARGER NEEDLES
32 STITCHES AND 20 ROWS = 4"/10 CM IN TWO-BY-TWO RIB
STITCH (UNSTRETCHED) WITH TWO STRANDS HELD
TOGETHER ON SMALLER NEEDLES

SPECIAL ARAN STITCHES
TWIST 2 BACK: SLIP THE NEXT STITCH ONTO CABLE
NEEDLE AND *HOLD AT BACK OF WORK,* KNIT NEXT
STITCH FROM LEFT-HAND NEEDLE, PURL STITCH FROM
CABLE NEEDLE.
TWIST 2 FRONT: SLIP THE NEXT STITCH ONTO CABLE
NEEDLE AND *HOLD IN FRONT OF WORK,* PURL NEXT
STITCH FROM LEFT-HAND NEEDLE, KNIT STITCH FROM
CABLE NEEDLE.

ZIGZAG-14 PATTERN

Row 1: Purl 5, [Twist 2 Back] 3 times, purl 3.

Row 2: Knit 4, [purl 1, knit 1] 3 times, knit 4.

Row 3: Purl 4, [Twist 2 Back] 3 times, purl 4.

Row 4: Knit 5, [purl 1, knit 1] 3 times, knit 3.

Row 5: Purl 3, [Twist 2 Back] 3 times, purl 5.

Row 6: Knit 6, [purl 1, knit 1] 3 times, knit 2.

Row 7: Purl 2, [Twist 2 Back] 3 times, purl 6.

Row 8: Knit 7, [purl 1, knit 1] 3 times, knit 1.

Row 9: Purl 1, [Twist 2 Back] 3 times, purl 7.

Row 10: Knit 8, [purl 1, knit 1] 3 times.

Row 11: [Twist 2 Back] 3 times, purl 8.

Row 12: Knit 9, [purl 1, knit 1] 2 times, purl 1.

Row 13: [Twist 2 Front] 3 times, purl 8.

Row 14: Knit 8 [purl 1, knit 1] 3 times.

Row 15: Purl 1, [Twist 2 Front] 3 times, purl 7.

Row 16: Knit 7, [purl 1, knit 1] 3 times, knit 1.

Row 17: Purl 2, [Twist 2 Front] 3 times, purl 6.

Row 18: Knit 6, [purl 1, knit 1] 3 times, knit 2.

Row 19: Purl 3, [Twist 2 Front] 3 times, purl 5.

Row 20: Knit 5, [purl 1, knit 1] 3 times, knit 3.

Row 21: Purl 4, [Twist 2 Front] 3 times, purl 4.

Row 22: Knit 4, [purl 1, knit 1] 3 times, knit 4.

Row 23: Purl 5, [Twist 2 Front] 3 times, purl 3.

Row 24: Knit 3, [purl 1, knit 1] 3 times, knit 5.

BACK

With larger needles, cast on 98 (102, 106) stitches with two strands of yarn held together. Work in stockinette stitch (knit all right-side rows and purl all wrong-side rows). Work 1 row even. Cast on 3 stitches at the beginning of the next 6 rows—116 (120, 124) stitches. Decrease 1 stitch at the beginning and end of every 6 rows 20 times—76 (80, 84) stitches. Work even until the piece measures 27½" (28", 28½")/70 (71, 72.5) cm.

ARMHOLE SHAPING

Bind off 4 stitches at the beginning of the next 2 rows—68 (72, 76) stitches. Decrease 1 stitch at the beginning and end of every other row 7 times—54 (58, 62) stitches. Work even until the piece measures 34" (35", 36")/86.5 (89, 91.5) cm.

SHOULDER SHAPING

Bind off 4 (5, 5) stitches at the beginning of the next 6 (4, 6) rows—30 (38, 32) stitches. Bind off 0 (4, 0) stitches at the beginning of the next 0 (2, 0) rows—30 (30, 32) stitches.

Bind off remaining stitches.

LEFT FRONT

With larger needles, cast on 52 (54, 56) stitches with two strands of yarn held together. Work in stockinette stitch. Work 1 row even. Cast on 3 stitches at the beginning of every right-side row 3 times—61 (63, 65) stitches. Decrease 1 stitch at the beginning of every 6 right-side rows 20 times—41 (43, 45) stitches.

ARMHOLE SHAPING

Bind off 4 stitches at the beginning of the next wrong-side row—37 (39, 41) stitches. Decrease 1 stitch at the beginning of every wrong-side row 7 times—30 (32, 34) stitches. Work even until the piece measures 34" (35", 36")/86.5 (89, 91.5) cm.

SHOULDER SHAPING

Bind off 4 (5, 5) stitches at the beginning of the next 3 (2, 3) wrong-side rows—18 (22, 19) stitches. Bind off 0 (4, 0) stitches at the beginning of the next 0 (1, 0) row—18 (18, 19) stitches.

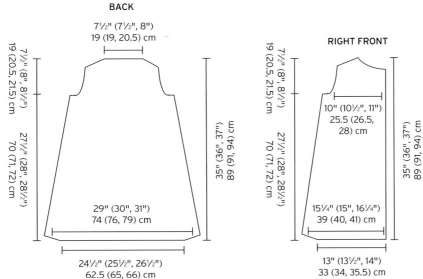

BACK

7½" (7½", 8")
19 (19, 20.5) cm

7½" (8", 8½")
19 (20.5, 21.5) cm

27½" (28", 28½")
70 (71, 72) cm

35" (36", 37")
89 (91, 94) cm

29" (30", 31")
74 (76, 79) cm

24½" (25½", 26½")
62.5 (65, 66) cm

RIGHT FRONT

7½" (8", 8½")
19 (20.5, 21.5) cm

10" (10½", 11")
25.5 (26.5, 28) cm

27½" (28", 28½")
70 (71, 72) cm

35" (36", 37")
89 (91, 94) cm

15¼" (15", 16¼")
39 (40, 41) cm

13" (13½", 14")
33 (34, 35.5) cm

RIGHT FRONT

Work as for the Left Front, but reverse shaping.

**SLEEVES
(Make two)**

With the larger needles, cast on 62 (66, 70) stitches for each sleeve with two strands of yarn held together. Work 3 (5, 7) stitches in stockinette stitch, work zigzag-14 pattern 4 times, work 3 (5, 7) stitches in stockinette stitch.

Repeat this row until sleeve measures 19" (20", 20½")/48 (51, 52) cm.

To shape sleeve cap, bind off 4 stitches at the beginning of the next 2 rows—54 (58, 62) stitches. Maintain zigzag-14 pattern as much as possible throughout cap shaping. Decrease 1 stitch at the beginning and end of every right-side row 7 times—40 (44, 48) stitches. Decrease 1 stitch at the beginning and end of every row 5 times—30 (34, 38) stitches.

Work 1 row even. Bind off remaining 30 (34, 38) stitches.

LEFT POCKET

With the larger needles, cast on 25 stitches with two strands of yarn held together. Work even in stockinette stitch for 5½"/14 cm, or approximately 28 rows, ending with a wrong-side row.

Decrease 1 stitch at the end of every right-side row 7 times—18 stitches. Decrease 1 stitch at the end of every right-side row and the beginning of every wrong-side row 7 times—11 stitches.

Bind off.

RIGHT POCKET

Make as for the Left Pocket, but reverse shaping.

LAPEL

With the smaller needles, cast on 20 stitches with two strands of yarn held together. Work in two-by-two rib stitch (knit 2, purl 2, repeat until the end of the row) until the lapel measures 92" (94", 96")/234 (239, 244) cm.

Bind off loosely in rib stitch pattern.

FINISHING

Weave in all loose ends with the tapestry needle.

With the tapestry needle and two strands of yarn, sew together the shoulder seams using backstitch. Sew together the side seams using backstitch. You may find it helpful to pin together the seams before sewing.

With the tapestry needle and two strands of yarn, seam together the Sleeves using backstitch. Pin Sleeves into armholes following the contours of the shaping. With the tapestry needle and two strands of yarn, sew the Sleeves into the armholes using backstitch.

HOOD

Pick up 40 stitches along the Right Front collar edge, 40 stitches along the Back neck edge, and 40 stitches along the Left Front collar edge—120 stitches total. Work in stockinette stitch until the hood measures 15"/38 cm from pickup row. Bind off. With the tapestry needle and two strands of yarn, sew the top seam of the hood using backstitch.

LAPEL Fold the Lapel in half lengthwise. Starting at the bottom hem of the Right Front, pin the lapel to the Right Front edge, along the front edge of the hood, and along the Left Front edge with the two halves, overlapping the side seam on the inside and outside edges by ½"/13 mm, or approximately 2 stitches (see photograph). Using the tapestry needle and two strands of yarn, whipstitch the Lapel to the body of the sweater using very small stitches so they will not be very noticeable when the garment is worn.

POCKETS With two strands of yarn, work a single crochet stitch around all the edges of both Pockets. Attach Pockets to side seams with large (1"/2.5 cm) whipstitch stitches around all the edges *except the straight edge,* which is lined up with the side seam.

BUTTONS With the crochet hook and two ends of yarn, make 6 chains, each approximately 5"/13 cm long. Try on the coat and place sewing pins where you would like to place the three buttons (see the photograph for placement suggestions). Each button should be approximately 1½"/3.8 cm from the edge of the lapel. Thread one of the chains through one of the wooden horn buttons, and with the tapestry needle and yarn tack down the yarn shank on the Left Front (see the photograph for guidance). Fold one of the other chains in half, and tack it down in a corresponding spot on the Right Front (see the photograph for guidance). Repeat these steps for the other two buttons and button loops.

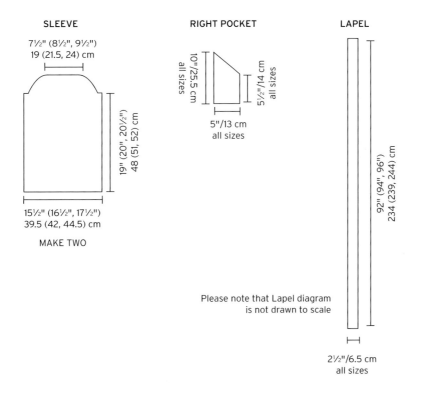

SLEEVE

7½" (8½", 9½")
19 (21.5, 24) cm

19" (20", 20½")
48 (51, 52) cm

15½" (16½", 17½")
39.5 (42, 44.5) cm

MAKE TWO

RIGHT POCKET

10"/25.5 cm
all sizes

5½"/14 cm
all sizes

5"/13 cm
all sizes

LAPEL

92" (94", 96")
234 (239, 244) cm

Please note that Lapel diagram
is not drawn to scale

2½"/6.5 cm
all sizes

ruffled bolero

A TUCK-STITCH, LACE-KNIT PATTERN COMBINED WITH A RUFFLED BORDER ALL AROUND CREATES A FEATHERY, ROMANTIC FEEL—AND THE SOFT YARN ADDS TO THAT EFFECT. THIS BOLERO LOOKS PERFECT OVER A SIMPLE DRESS. CLOSE IT WITH A BEAUTIFUL PIN FOR AN EVEN MORE FINISHED LOOK.

SIZES
SMALL (MEDIUM, LARGE)

FINISHED MEASUREMENTS
CHEST: 36" (38", 40")/91.5 (96.5, 101.5) CM
LENGTH: 13" (14", 15")/33 (35.5, 38) CM

YARN
3 (3, 3) SKEINS SUSS FISHNET (53% ACRYLIC/30% NYLON/
   17% ALPACA; 1.5 OUNCES/43 GRAMS; 285 YARDS/261
   METERS), COLOR BROWN

NOTIONS
1 PAIR SIZE 10 (6 MM) CIRCULAR NEEDLES, 32"/81 CM LONG
4 STITCH MARKERS (OPTIONAL)
1 TAPESTRY NEEDLE
SEWING PINS

GAUGE
12 STITCHES AND 20 ROWS = 4"/10 CM IN LACE PATTERN
   (DESCRIBED BELOW)
12 STITCHES AND 18 ROWS = 4"/10 CM IN STOCKINETTE
   STITCH

SPECIAL STITCH
TUCK STITCH: BRING THE WORKING YARN TO THE FRONT.
   INSERT THE RIGHT-HAND NEEDLE THROUGH THE STITCH
   TWO ROWS BELOW AND PURL THE STITCH, DROPPING
   THE OTHER TWO STITCHES (THE ONE ABOVE AND THE
   ONE ON THE LEFT-HAND NEEDLE) FROM THE LEFT-HAND
   NEEDLE AS IF YOU HAD PURLED THEM TOO.

**4-ROW
TUCK-STITCH
LACE PATTERN**

Rows 1 and 3 (right side): Purl all stitches.

Row 2 (wrong side): Knit all stitches.

Row 4: *Knit 2, tuck stitch*; repeat from * to * across row.

Repeat Rows 1–4.

BACK

Cast on 42 (46, 48) stitches. Work in tuck-stitch lace pattern.

Increase 1 stitch at the beginning and end of every 5 rows 6 times—54 (58, 60) stitches. Work even until the piece measures 6½" (7½", 8")/16.5 (19, 20.5) cm from the cast-on edge, ending with a wrong-side row. Place stitch markers or tie contrasting pieces of yarn at the beginning and end of this row.

Increase 1 stitch at the beginning and end of every 3 rows 9 times—72 (76, 78) stitches. Work even until the piece measures 5½" (5½", 6")/14 (14, 15) cm from the stitch markers.

Bind off 13 (14, 14) stitches at the beginning of the next 2 rows—46 (48, 50) stitches. Bind off 12 (13, 13) stitches at the beginning of the next 2 rows—22 (22, 24) stitches remain.

Bind off all stitches.

LEFT FRONT

Cast on 19 (21, 22) stitches. Work in tuck-stitch lace pattern. The Front pieces are worked with two different rates of increases and decreases. Instructions are given for the side seam edge first and then the center edge, but when working this piece, the shaping must be done at the same time.

On side seam (right) edge, increase 1 stitch every 5 rows 6 times. Work even until the piece measures 6½" (7½", 8")/16.5 (19, 20.5) cm from the cast-on edge, ending with a wrong-side row. Place a stitch marker or tie a contrasting piece of yarn (see diagram).

To shape sleeves, increase 1 stitch every 3 rows 9 times. Work even until the piece measures 5½" (5½", 6")/14 (14, 15) cm from the stitch marker.

To shape shoulders, bind off 13 (14, 14) stitches at the beginning of the next side seam edge row. Bind off 12 (13, 13) stitches at the beginning of the next side seam edge row.

At the same time, on the center edge, increase 1 stitch every 3 rows 7 (9, 9) times. Work even until the piece measures 6½" (6¾", 7½")/16.5 (17, 19) cm. Decrease 1 stitch every 2 rows 16 (18, 19) times. Work even until bind-off.

RIGHT FRONT   Work as for the Left Front, but reverse shaping.

SLEEVE RUFFLES (Make two)   Cast on 60 (60, 66) stitches. Work in stockinette stitch (knit all right-side rows and purl all wrong-side rows) for 10 rows.

Bind off *loosely.*

RUFFLED EDGING (Make two)   Cast on 135 (135, 138) stitches. Work in stockinette stitch for 10 rows.

Bind off *loosely.*

FINISHING   Weave in all loose ends with the tapestry needle.

Place the Front and the Back piece together with right (purl) sides facing each other and pin shoulder seams. With the tapestry needle and yarn, sew together the shoulder seams using backstitch. With the tapestry needle and yarn, sew together the side seams using backstitch. Use the stitch markers to tell you where the sleeve shaping begins.

SLEEVE RUFFLES   With the tapestry needle and yarn, work a loose running stitch through the cast-on edge of one of the Sleeve Ruffles. Measure the length of the armhole and gather the Sleeve Ruffle to that length. Tie off yarn. Start at the armhole and pin the Sleeve Ruffle in place.

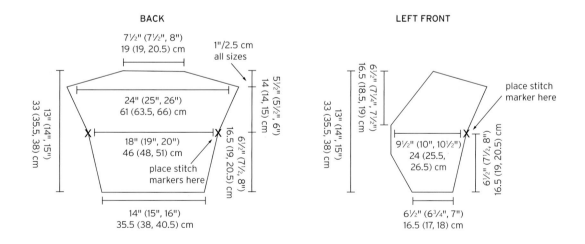

You may find it helpful to turn the garment inside out to do this. With the tapestry needle and yarn, sew the ruffle into the armhole. Whipstitch the two narrow ends of the Sleeve Ruffle together at the armhole.

Repeat for the second Sleeve Ruffle.

RUFFLED EDGING   Pin one end of one of the Ruffled Edging pieces to the center of the Back neck and one to the center of the bottom (cast-on) edge of the Back. Be careful not to twist the ruffle. Work the ruffle around the edge of the bolero top, gathering and pinning it in place as you go. With the tapestry needle and yarn, sew the Ruffled Edging to the bolero.

Repeat this process for the second Ruffled Edging piece and the other half of the bolero.

Whipstitch the two narrow ends of the Ruffled Edging pieces together at the back of the neck and the center of the bottom hem of the Back.

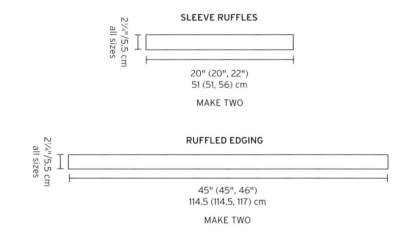

SLEEVE RUFFLES

2¼"/5.5 cm all sizes

20" (20", 22")
51 (51, 56) cm

MAKE TWO

RUFFLED EDGING

2¼"/5.5 cm all sizes

45" (45", 46")
114.5 (114.5, 117) cm

MAKE TWO

swing capelet with collar

I FIND SO MANY GREAT IDEAS WHEN I EXPLORE THRIFT SHOPS. AN OLD BROWN VELVET VINTAGE CAPE FROM THE FIFTIES WAS THE INSPIRATION FOR THIS SWINGY VERSION IN AN IRIDESCENT OFF-WHITE YARN. BECAUSE IT CLOSES WITH JUST ONE HUGE BUTTON AT THE COLLAR, IT FALLS OPEN AND REALLY MOVES WITH YOU. PUT IT ON AND YOU'RE READY FOR AN EVENING THEATER SHOW.

SIZE
ONE SIZE FITS MOST (SEE FINISHED MEASUREMENTS)

FINISHED MEASUREMENTS
CHEST: 38"/96.5 CM
LENGTH: 17¾"/45 CM

YARN
10 SKEINS SUSS BUTTERFLY (50% COTTON/50%
    POLYAMIDE; 2 OUNCES/57 GRAMS; 52 YARDS/48
    METERS), COLOR NATURAL

NOTIONS
1 PAIR SIZE 13 (9 MM) CIRCULAR NEEDLES, 24"/61 CM LONG
    (OR SIZE TO OBTAIN GAUGE)
KNITTING ROW COUNTER (RECOMMENDED)
1 LARGE STITCH HOLDER
1 LARGE TAPESTRY NEEDLE
1 SIZE H (5 MM) CROCHET HOOK
1 ABALONE SHELL BUTTON, 2"/5 CM IN DIAMETER
    (AVAILABLE FROM WWW.SUSSDESIGN.COM)
SEWING NEEDLE AND IVORY-COLORED THREAD

GAUGE
10 STITCHES AND 13 ROWS = 4"/10 CM IN STOCKINETTE
    STITCH

BACK

Cast on 58 stitches. Work even in stockinette stitch for 4½"/11.5 cm, or approximately 14 rows, ending with a wrong-side row.

Bind off 2 stitches at the beginning of the next 2 rows—54 stitches. Decrease 1 stitch at the beginning and end of every 4 rows 7 times—40 stitches. Decrease 1 stitch at the beginning and end of every row 12 times—16 stitches. Work even for 2 rows—58 rows.

Place remaining 16 stitches on stitch holder.

LEFT FRONT

Cast on 32 stitches. Work even in stockinette stitch for 4½"/11.5 cm, or approximately 14 rows, ending with a wrong-side row. Bind off 2 stitches at the beginning of the next right-side row—30 stitches.

From this point on, the side edge and lapel edge shaping are worked at different rates. When the right side of the piece is facing you, the side edge is the right-hand edge and the lapel edge is the left-hand edge.

Decrease 1 stitch every 4 rows 7 times. Decrease 1 stitch every row for 12 rows.

At the same time, work even until the piece measures 13¾"/35 cm, ending with a right-side row. Bind off 5 stitches at the beginning of the next wrong-side row. Decrease 1 stitch at the beginning of every wrong-side row 5 times.

Work until you have 58 rows. Bind off remaining 1 stitch.

RIGHT FRONT

Work as for the Left Front, but reverse shaping.

At the same time, when the piece measures 10½"/26.5 cm from the cast-on edge, make a buttonhole as follows on the first right-side row:

Row 1: Knit 3 stitches, join second ball of yarn, and work as directed for that row.

Rows 2–4: Work shaping as directed, but continue to work from two balls of yarn.

Row 5: Tie off second ball of yarn, work all stitches from first ball of yarn, and continue piece as directed.

SLEEVES
(Make two)

Cast on 48 stitches. Work even in stockinette stitch for 5"/12.5 cm, or approximately 16 rows.

Bind off 2 stitches at the beginning of the next 2 rows—44 stitches.

Decrease 1 stitch at the beginning and end of every 4 rows 7 times—30 stitches. Decrease 1 stitch at the beginning and end of every row 12 times—6 stitches.

Work even for 2 rows—58 rows.

Bind off all stitches.

FINISHING

Weave in all loose ends with the tapestry needle.

Pin together the side seams and, with the tapestry needle and yarn, sew the side seams using backstitch. Pin together and sew the sleeve seams using backstitch. Pin the Sleeves to the body of the coat and sew the Sleeves to the body using backstitch.

COLLAR

Pick up 12 stitches along the Left Front collar neckline, 6 stitches from the left Sleeve cap, 16 stitches from the stitch holder on the Back neck, 6 stitches from the right Sleeve cap, and 12 stitches from the Right Front collar neckline—52 stitches total. Work even in stockinette stitch for 7"/18 cm. Make sure that the right side (knit side) of the collar is facing the inside so it will be showing on the outside of the coat when the collar is turned over and worn. Bind off loosely.

With the crochet hook, start at the bottom edge of the Left Front and work a single crochet stitch up the lapel of the Left Front, around the edge of the collar and down the lapel edge of the Right Front. Fasten off.

Work a single crochet around the buttonhole.

With the sewing needle and thread, sew on the button.

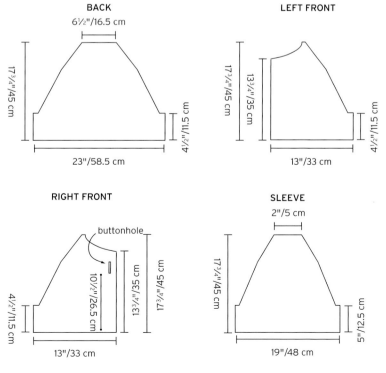

BACK
6½"/16.5 cm
17¾"/45 cm
4½"/11.5 cm
23"/58.5 cm

LEFT FRONT
17¾"/45 cm
13¾"/35 cm
4½"/11.5 cm
13"/33 cm

RIGHT FRONT
buttonhole
4½"/11.5 cm
10½"/26.5 cm
13¾"/35 cm
17¾"/45 cm
13"/33 cm

SLEEVE
2"/5 cm
17¾"/45 cm
5"/12.5 cm
19"/48 cm
MAKE TWO

open-front cape

THIS FORTIES-INSPIRED PIECE HAS SUCH A CLASSIC LOOK TO IT. I PICTURE KATHARINE HEPBURN IN IT, WEARING LONG BLACK GLOVES, A PENCIL SKIRT, AND HIGH HEELS. THIS TAUPISH-COLORED CAPE GOES WITH EVERYTHING. IT WOULD ALSO BE BEAUTIFUL IN BLACK.

SIZES
ONE SIZE FITS MOST

FINISHED MEASUREMENTS
CHEST: FITS CHEST UP TO 40"/101.5 CM
LENGTH: 32"/81 CM (INCLUDING COLLAR)

YARNS
A: 13 (13, 14) SKEINS SUSS RUSTIC (80% WOOL/
15% POLYAMIDE/3% COTTON/2% ACRYLIC; 2 OUNCES/
57 GRAMS; 85 YARDS/78 METERS), COLOR OYSTER
B: 1 SKEIN SUSS MOHAIR (76.5% COTTON/17.5% WOOL/
6% NYLON; 1.5 OUNCES/43 GRAMS; 126 YARDS/
115 METERS), COLOR NATURAL

NOTIONS
1 PAIR SIZE 10 (6 MM) CIRCULAR NEEDLES, 32"/81 CM LONG
1 PAIR SIZE 9 (5.5 MM) CIRCULAR NEEDLES, 24"/61 CM LONG
1 LARGE TAPESTRY NEEDLE
SEWING NEEDLE AND BROWN THREAD
4 TORTOISESHELL PLASTIC BUTTONS, 7/8"/2.2 CM
IN DIAMETER

GAUGE
16 STITCHES AND 20 ROWS = 4"/10 CM IN STOCKINETTE
STITCH WITH YARN A AND SMALLER NEEDLES
18 STITCHES AND 20 ROWS = 4"/10 CM IN TWO-BY-TWO RIB
STITCH WITH YARN A AND LARGER NEEDLES

BACK

Cast on 112 stitches with yarn A and the larger needles. Work in two-by-two rib stitch (knit 2, purl 2, repeat until the end of the row) for 10 rows.

Switch to the smaller needles. Work in stockinette stitch (knit all right-side rows and purl all wrong-side rows). Decrease 1 stitch at the beginning and end of every 10 rows 8 times— 96 stitches total. Decrease 1 stitch at the beginning and end of every 4 rows 9 times—78 stitches total. Work even until the piece measures 26"/66 cm, ending with a wrong-side row.

COLLAR SHAPING

On the next (right-side) row, knit 1, *knit 2 stitches together*; repeat from * to * until 1 stitch remains, knit 1 stitch—40 stitches remain. Work even for 6 rows. Decrease 2 stitches at the beginning of the next 6 rows—28 stitches remain. Work even until the piece measures 32"/81 cm from the cast-on edge.

Bind off loosely.

LEFT FRONT

Cast on 56 stitches with the larger needles. Work in two-by-two rib stitch for 10 rows.

Switch to smaller needles. Work in stockinette stitch.

On the left (lapel) edge, work even until the piece measures 9"/23 cm from the cast-on edge, ending with a right-side row. On the next wrong-side row, work 28 stitches, join a second ball of yarn, and work remaining stitches from this second ball. Work from two balls for 8"/20.5 cm. At the next wrong-side row, work across all stitches from first ball of yarn. Cut yarn from the second ball. Work even until bind-off.

At the same time, on the right (side seam) edge, decrease 1 stitch every 10 rows 8 times— 48 stitches total. Decrease 1 stitch at the beginning of every 4 rows on the side seam edge 9 times—39 stitches total. Work even until the piece measures 26"/66 cm, ending with a right-side row.

COLLAR SHAPING

On the next (wrong-side) row: [Purl 1, purl 2 stitches together] across entire row—26 stitches remain. Work 6 rows even. Decrease 2 stitches at the beginning of every right-side row 3 times—20 stitches total. Work even until the piece measures 32"/81 cm from the cast-on edge.

Bind off loosely.

RIGHT FRONT   Work as for the Left Front, but reverse shaping.

FINISHING   Weave in all loose ends with the tapestry needle.

Place the Front and Back pieces together with the right sides facing each other and pin together the shoulder and side seams. With the tapestry needle and yarn A, sew together the shoulder and side seams using backstitch.

BUTTON BAND   Start at the top of the turtleneck collar and, with the larger needles, pick up 144 stitches with yarn A along the Left Front straight edge. Work in two-by-two rib stitch for 12 rows. Bind off loosely in rib pattern.

BUTTONHOLE BAND   Start at the bottom hem and, with the larger needles, pick up 144 stitches with yarn A along the Right Front straight edge. Work in two-by-two rib stitch. Work even for 6 rows (working yarn should be at top of collar now).

Work a buttonhole row as follows: Work 5 stitches, yarn over, work 2 stitches together, [work 14 stitches, yarn over, work 2 stitches together] 3 times, work remaining 89 stitches. Work 5 rows in two-by-two rib stitch. Bind off loosely in rib pattern.

Place the Right Front piece over the Left Front piece so the two center bands are lined up evenly. With the sewing pins, mark the spots on the Left Front button band where the 4 buttons should be attached. With the sewing needle and thread, attach a button at each spot marked by the pins.

With the tapestry needle and two strands of yarn B, work a running stitch from the bottom of one of the hand openings to the two-by-two rib edging. Each stitch should be approximately ½"/13 mm long. Work another running stitch from the top of the hand opening to the beginning of the turtleneck collar. Repeat for the second hand opening.

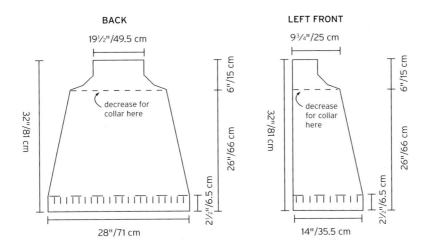

knitted denim jacket

THE DENIM JACKET IS A FASHION STAPLE. THIS STRETCHY KNIT VERSION LETS YOU ENJOY THAT CLASSIC LOOK WITHOUT THE STIFFNESS OF DENIM. I LOVE THE CUTE TOPSTITCHED DETAILS, AND THE CREAM AND CHOCOLATE LOOKS WONDERFUL WITH JEANS.

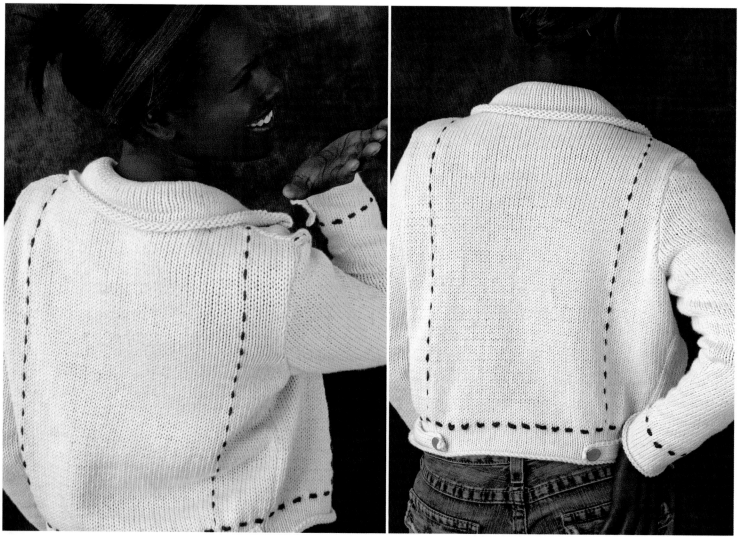

SIZES
SMALL (MEDIUM, LARGE, EXTRA-LARGE)

FINISHED MEASUREMENTS
CHEST: 40" (42", 44", 46")/101.5 (106.5, 112, 117) CM
LENGTH: 20" (21", 22", 23")/51 (53.5, 56, 58.5) CM

YARNS
A: 6 (6, 7, 8) SKEINS SUSS BOMULL (100% COTTON;
4 OUNCES/114 GRAMS; 190 YARDS/174 METERS),
COLOR ECRU
B: 1 SKEIN SUSS COTTON (100% COTTON; 2.5 OUNCES/
71 GRAMS; 118 YARDS/108 METERS), COLOR CHOCOLATE

NOTIONS
1 PAIR SIZE 9 (5.5 MM) NEEDLES
1 LARGE TAPESTRY NEEDLE
1 SIZE G (4 MM) CROCHET HOOK
SEWING PINS
SEWING NEEDLE AND ECRU THREAD
11 BRUSHED METAL BUTTONS WITH SHANKS, ¾"/2 CM
IN DIAMETER

GAUGE
16 STITCHES AND 20 ROWS = 4"/10 CM IN STOCKINETTE
STITCH WITH YARN A

BACK

Cast on 58 (62, 66, 70) stitches with yarn A. Work in stockinette stitch (knit all right-side rows and purl all wrong-side rows). Work even for 12 rows.

Increase 6 stitches evenly across the next row—64 (68, 72, 76) stitches. Increase 1 stitch at the beginning and end of every 4 (5, 5, 6) rows 8 times—80 (84, 88, 92) stitches. Work even until the piece measures 10" (10½", 11", 12")/25.5 (26.5, 28, 30.5) cm from the cast-on edge, ending with a wrong-side row.

ARMHOLE SHAPING

Bind off 4 stitches at the beginning of the next 2 rows—72 (76, 80, 84) stitches. Decrease 1 stitch at the beginning and end of every wrong-side row 6 (6, 7, 8) times—60 (64, 66, 68) stitches. Work even until the piece measures 18½" (19½", 20½", 21½")/47 (49.5, 52, 54.5) cm from the cast-on edge, ending with a wrong-side row.

SHOULDER SHAPING

Bind off 5 stitches at the beginning of the next 4 (8, 8, 8) rows—40 (24, 26, 28) stitches. Bind off 4 (0, 0, 0) stitches at the beginning of the next 4 (0, 0, 0) rows—24 (24, 26, 28) stitches remain.

Bind off all remaining stitches.

LEFT FRONT

Cast on 32 (34, 36, 38) stitches with yarn A. Work even in stockinette stitch for 12 rows.

Increase 3 stitches evenly across the next row—35 (37, 39, 41) stitches. Increase 1 stitch at the beginning of every 4 (5, 5, 6) rows on the right (side seam) edge 8 times—43 (45, 47, 49) stitches. Work even until the piece measures 10" (10½", 11", 12")/25.5 (26.5, 28, 30.5) cm from the cast-on edge, ending with a wrong-side row.

ARMHOLE SHAPING

Bind off 4 stitches at the beginning of the next right-side row—39 (41, 43, 45) stitches. Decrease 1 stitch at the end of every wrong-side row 6 (6, 7, 8) times—33 (35, 36, 37) stitches. Work even until the piece measures 18½" (19½", 20½", 21½")/47 (49.5, 52, 54.5) cm from the cast-on edge, ending with a wrong-side row.

SHOULDER SHAPING

Bind off 5 stitches at the beginning of the next 2 (4, 4, 4) right-side rows. Bind off 4 (0, 0, 0) stitches at the beginning of the next 2 (0, 0, 0) right-side rows.

NECKLINE

At the same time, when the piece measures 16" (17", 18", 19")/40.5 (43, 46, 48) cm from the cast-on edge, bind off 5 stitches at the beginning of the next wrong-side row. Decrease 1 stitch at the beginning of every wrong-side row and end of every right side row for 10 (10, 11, 12) rows. Work even until shoulder seam bind-off.

RIGHT FRONT

Work as for the Left Front, but reverse shaping.

At the same time, work buttonhole rows as follows:

When the piece measures 1"/2.5 cm from the cast-on edge, ending with a right-side row, purl 6, yarn over, purl 2 stitches together, purl remaining stitches.

When the piece measures 4½" (4¾", 5", 5 ¼")/11.5 (12, 12.5, 13.5) cm from the cast-on edge, ending with a right-side row, purl 6, yarn over, purl 2 stitches together, purl remaining stitches.

When the piece measures 8" (8½", 9", 9½")/20.5 (21.5, 23, 24) cm from the cast-on edge, ending with a right-side row, purl 6, yarn over, purl 2 stitches together, purl remaining stitches.

When the piece measures 11½" (12 ¼", 13", 13¾")/29 (31, 33, 35) cm from the cast-on edge, ending with a right-side row, purl 6, yarn over, purl 2 together, purl remaining stitches.

When the piece measures 15" (16", 17", 18")/38 (40.5, 43, 46) cm from the cast-on edge, ending with a right-side row, purl 6, yarn over, purl 2 together, purl remaining stitches.

LEFT FRONT BUTTON BAND

Cast on 12 stitches with yarn A. Work even in stockinette stitch until the piece measures 16" (17", 18", 19")/40.5 (43, 46, 48) cm from the cast-on edge, ending with a wrong-side row.

Bind off 7 stitches at the beginning of the next right-side row—5 stitches remain. Decrease 1 stitch at the end of every wrong-side row and the beginning of every right-side row for 4 rows. Bind off the remaining stitch.

RIGHT FRONT BUTTON BAND

Work as for the Left Front Button Band, but reverse shaping.

At the same time, work buttonholes as for the Right Front.

SLEEVES (Make two)

Cast on 41 (45, 49, 49) stitches with yarn A. Work in stockinette stitch. Work even for 6 rows. Work an eyelet row as follows: Work until 6 stitches remain, yarn over, work 2 stitches together, work remaining 4 stitches. Work even for 6 rows—13 rows total.

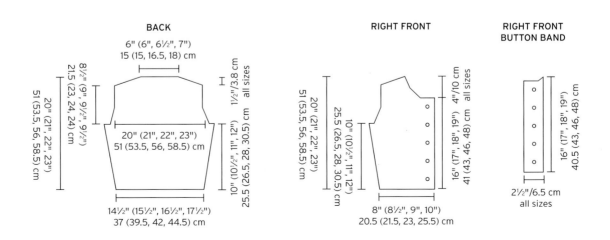

Bind off 7 stitches at the beginning of the next wrong-side row—34 (38, 42, 42) stitches. Increase 1 stitch at the beginning and end of every 8 rows 10 (10, 10, 11) times—54 (58, 62, 64) stitches. Work even until the piece measures 19 (20", 20", 20½")/48 (51, 51, 52) cm.

To shape armholes, bind off 4 stitches at the beginning of the next 2 rows—46 (50, 54, 56) stitches. Decrease 1 stitch at the beginning and end of every wrong-side row 8 times—30 (34, 38, 40) stitches. Decrease 1 stitch at the beginning and end of every row 5 (5, 6, 6) times—20 (24, 26, 28) stitches.

Bind off all remaining stitches.

COLLAR

Cast on 70 (70, 72, 76) stitches with yarn A. Work in stockinette stitch. Decrease 1 stitch at the beginning and end of every 4 rows 5 times—60 (60, 62, 66) stitches. Work even for 2 rows.

Bind off 5 stitches at the beginning of every row for 6 rows—30 (30, 32, 36) stitches.

Bind off.

POCKET COVERS (Make two)

Cast on 17 stitches with yarn A. Work even in stockinette stitch for 8 rows. Work an eyelet row as follows: Work 8 stitches, yarn over, work 2 stitches together, work remaining 7 stitches. Work 2 rows even.

Decrease 1 stitch at the beginning and end of every wrong-side row 8 times.

Bind off remaining stitch.

DECORATIVE STRAPS (Make two)

Cast on 6 stitches with yarn A. Work even in stockinette stitch for 20 rows. Decrease 1 stitch at the beginning of the next 5 rows. Bind off remaining stitch.

FINISHING

Weave in all loose ends with the tapestry needle.

With the tapestry needle and yarn, whipstitch the Button Bands to the wrong side of the Left and Right Front, lining up the buttonholes as a guide for the Right Front Button Band. As you sew the jacket together, you may find it helpful to pin the pieces in place first. Use very small stitches and make sure the stitches are not visible from the right side. You can also use the sewing needle and thread if you want to make sure your stitches remain invisible.

With the tapestry needle and yarn A, sew together the shoulder and side seams using backstitch. Fold the Sleeves in half lengthwise with the right sides facing each other and, with the tapestry needle and yarn A, sew the sleeve seams using backstitch. Leave the small buttonhole cuff unseamed.

With the tapestry needle and yarn A, whipstitch the Decorative Straps to the Back waistband at the side seams approximately ½"/13 mm from the bottom hem of the jacket. The pointed tip should be facing away from the side seam. With the sewing needle and thread, sew a button to each strap (see diagram).

Starting at the center of the Back neck, pin the Collar into place so the right side will be showing when garment is worn. The Collar will be set back approximately 1"/2.5 cm from the front center edges. With the crochet hook and yarn A, work a single crochet stitch join on the *outside* of the jacket to attach Collar.

BUTTONS	Lay the jacket flat with the Right Front over the Left Front. With the straight pins, use the placement of the buttonholes to mark the spots where the buttons should be attached. With the sewing needle and thread, attach a button at each of these five spots, removing the pins as you go.

Use the same technique to mark the spot where the button should be attached on each sleeve cuff. With the tapestry needle and thread, attach one button to each of the sleeve cuffs. |
| DECORATIVE STITCHING | With the tapestry needle and two strands of yarn B, work a running stitch around the top edge of the waistband and sleeve cuffs. Each stitch should be approximately ½"/13 mm long. Work a running stitch around the armhole approximately ¼"/6 mm from the armhole seam.

Start at the bottom hem of the Back 3"/7.5 cm from the right side seam and, with the tapestry needle and two strands of yarn B, work a running stitch straight up the Back and down the Right Front. Use the line of knitted stitches to guide you. Repeat at the left side seam of the Back and Left Front.

Approximately 6"/15 cm from the top shoulder seam of the Right Front, work a horizontal running stitch from the armhole seam to the center edge. Repeat for the Left Front.

Refer to the photograph for stitching suggestions, but feel free to add these great running stitches wherever you might see decorative topstitching on a classic denim jacket. |
| POCKETS | With the tapestry needle and yarn A, backstitch the top edge of one of the Pocket Covers to the Left Front approximately ½"/13 mm below the horizontal running stitch and 1"/2.5 cm from the armhole seam. Repeat for the second Pocket Cover and the Right Front.

With the sewing needle and thread, attach one button to the Left Front and one to the Right Front where indicated by the Pocket Cover placement. |

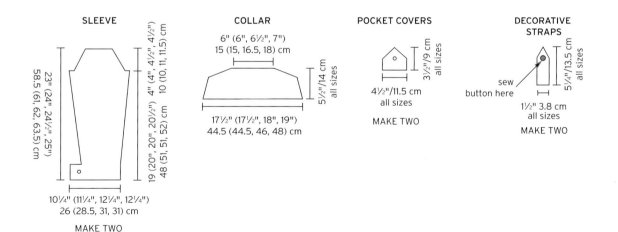

SLEEVE

23" (24", 24½", 25")
58.5 (61, 62, 63.5) cm

4" (4", 4½", 4½")
10 (10, 11, 11.5) cm

19 (20", 20", 20½")
48 (51, 51, 52) cm

10¼" (11¼", 12¼", 12¼")
26 (28.5, 31, 31) cm

MAKE TWO

COLLAR

6" (6", 6½", 7")
15 (15, 16.5, 18) cm

5½"/14 cm
all sizes

17½" (17½", 18", 19")
44.5 (44.5, 46, 48) cm

POCKET COVERS

3½"/9 cm
all sizes

4½"/11.5 cm
all sizes

MAKE TWO

DECORATIVE STRAPS

5¼"/13.5 cm
all sizes

sew button here

1½" 3.8 cm
all sizes

MAKE TWO

fuzzy scarf coat with bell sleeves

I USED TO HAVE A RED FORD MUSTANG CONVERTIBLE WITH BLACK LEATHER SEATS. WHEN I DROVE AROUND L.A. WEARING THIS COAT, KNIT IN WHITE, THE SCARF WOULD WAVE BEHIND ME IN THE BREEZE. I FELT SO CAREFREE. NO WONDER JULIA ROBERTS AND SANDRA BULLOCK HAVE BOTH BOUGHT THIS DESIGN IN TRADITIONAL BLACK. THE ONE PICTURED HERE IS MADE IN A TEXTURED BLEND YARN.

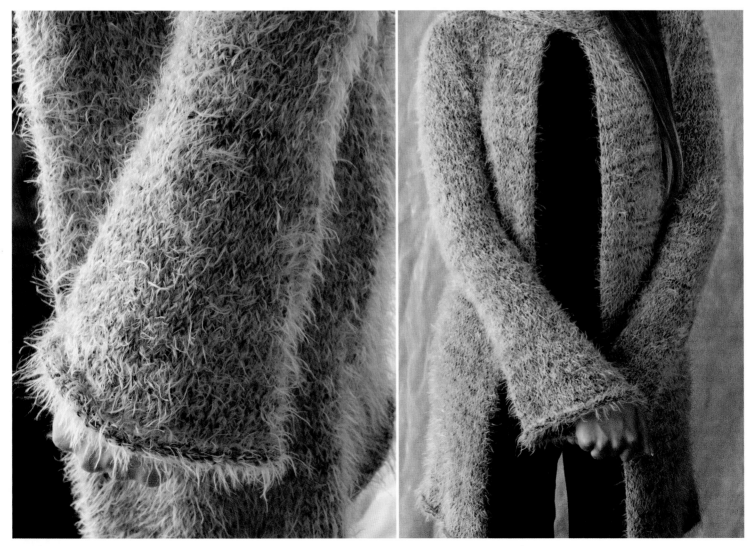

SIZES
SMALL (MEDIUM, LARGE)

FINISHED MEASUREMENTS
CHEST: 38" (40", 42")/96.5 (101.5, 106.5) CM
LENGTH: 31" (32", 33")/79 (81, 84) CM

YARN
18 (19, 20) SKEINS SUSS ROYAL (45% NYLON/35% VISCOSE/
    15% ACRYLIC/5% ALPACA; 2 OUNCES/57 GRAMS;
    102 YARDS/93 METERS), COLOR LAPIS

NOTIONS
1 PAIR SIZE 9 (5.5 MM) CIRCULAR NEEDLES, 24"/61 CM LONG
1 KNITTING ROW COUNTER (RECOMMENDED)
1 LARGE TAPESTRY NEEDLE
SEWING PINS

GAUGE
16 STITCHES AND 20 ROWS = 4"/10 CM IN
    STOCKINETTE STITCH

BACK

Cast on 76 (80, 84) stitches. Work even in stockinette stitch (knit all right-side rows and purl all wrong-side rows) until the piece measures 25" (25½", 26")/63.5 (65, 66) cm, or approximately 124 (128, 130) rows, ending with a wrong-side row.

ARMHOLE SHAPING

Bind off 4 stitches at the beginning of the next 2 rows—68 (72, 76) stitches. Decrease 1 stitch at the beginning and end of every other row 6 times—56 (60, 64) stitches. Work even until the piece measures 29½" (30½", 31½")/75 (77.5, 80) cm from the cast-on edge, ending with a wrong-side row.

SHOULDER SHAPING

Bind off 4 (4, 5) stitches at the beginning of the next 4 (6, 2) rows—40 (36, 54) stitches. Bind off 3 (3, 4) stitches at the beginning of the next 4 (2, 6) rows—28 (30, 30) stitches.

Bind off all stitches.

LEFT FRONT

Cast on 50 (52, 54) stitches.

Work even in stockinette stitch until the piece measures 21½" (22½", 23½") 54.5 (57, 59.5) cm, ending with a right-side row. From this point on, the neckline and the armhole/ shoulder will be shaped at different rates. The neckline shaping is on the left edge of the piece when the right side is facing you, while the armhole and shoulder shaping are on the right edge of the piece when the right side is facing you.

Decrease 1 stitch at the beginning of the next wrong-side row and every 8 wrong-side rows 4 times—5 stitches total decreased. Work 7 rows even. Bind off 7 (8, 8) stitches at the beginning of the next wrong-side row. Decrease 1 stitch at the beginning of every row 15 times.

At the same time, work even until the piece measures 25" (25½", 26")/63.5 (65, 66) cm, or approximately 124 (128, 130) rows, ending with a wrong-side row. Bind off 4 stitches at the beginning of the next right-side row. Decrease 1 stitch at the beginning of the next 6 right-side rows.

Bind off 4 (4, 5) stitches at the beginning of the next 2 (3, 1) right-side row(s). Bind off 3 (3, 4) stitches at the beginning of the next 2 (1, 3) right-side rows. Work 1 row even.

Bind off remaining stitches.

RIGHT FRONT

Work as for the Left Front, but reverse shaping.

SLEEVES (Make two)

Cast on 56 (60, 64) stitches. Work sleeve in stockinette stitch. Decrease 1 stitch at the beginning and end of every 12 (12, 14) rows 6 times—44 (48, 52) stitches. Work even until the piece measures 18½″ (18½″, 20″)/47 (47, 51) cm.

To shape cap, bind off 4 stitches at the beginning of the next two rows—36 (40, 44) stitches. Decrease 1 stitch at the beginning and end of every other row 8 times—20 (24, 28) stitches. Decrease 1 stitch at the beginning and end of every row 6 times—8 (12, 16) stitches.

Bind off.

SCARF

Cast on 36 stitches. Work in stockinette stitch until the piece measures 60″/152.5 cm (approximately 300 rows).

Bind off.

FINISHING

Weave in all loose ends with the tapestry needle.

Place the Front and Back pieces together with their right sides facing each other. With the tapestry needle and yarn, sew together the shoulder seams using backstitch.

With the tapestry needle and yarn, sew up the side seams using backstitch. Fold the Sleeves in half with the right sides facing each other and sew up the sleeve seams using backstitch.

Pin the Sleeves into the armholes, following the contours of the shaping. You may find it helpful to turn the piece inside out to do this. Make sure you pin the Sleeves evenly so there is no bunching or stretching. Sew the Sleeves into the armholes.

With the right sides facing each other, fold the Scarf in half widthwise to find the center and place a sewing pin at this point (see diagram). Fold the coat in half lengthwise and mark the center point of the Back neck with a sewing pin (see diagram). Attach the center point of the Scarf to this Back neck center point. Make sure that the right (stockinette) side of the Scarf is facing outward. With the tapestry needle and yarn, start at that center point and attach the Scarf to the Back of the neck and the Front collar edge.

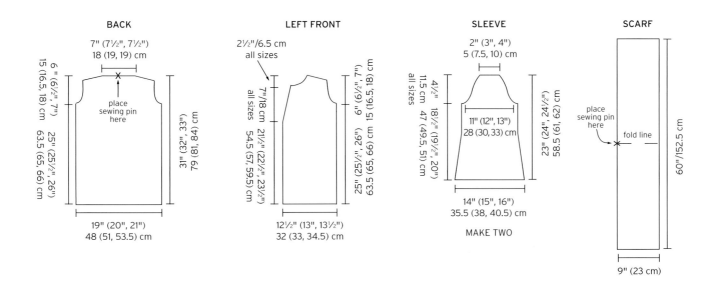

accessories

slinky scarf

YOU DON'T WEAR THIS SCARF FOR WARMTH! IT'S TO ADD THAT TOUCH OF COLOR AND GLAMOUR WHEN YOU'RE DRESSING UP FOR A SPECIAL OCCASION. YOU KNIT A SHINY BOUCLÉ YARN IN A SIMPLE STOCKINETTE, THEN ENHANCE IT WITH TEXTURE BY WEAVING RIBBON OR A CHUNKY WOOL THROUGHOUT. I CHOSE A RICH BURGUNDY, BUT THIS DESIGN WOULD LOOK PRETTY IN ANY COLOR. IT WOULD ALSO MAKE A GREAT GIFT.

SIZE
ONE SIZE FITS ALL

FINISHED MEASUREMENTS
15" WIDE X 85" LONG/38 CM X 216 CM

YARN
A: 3 SKEINS SUSS SHINE (100% RAYON; 1 OUNCE/28;
   136 YARDS/124M), COLOR BLACK CHERRY
B: ANY BULKY WOOL OR RIBBON OF YOUR CHOICE

NOTIONS
1 PAIR SIZE 11 (8 MM) NEEDLES
1 LARGE TAPESTRY NEEDLE
SEWING PINS OR SAFETY PINS

GAUGE
12 STITCHES AND 16 ROWS = 4"/10 CM IN
   STOCKINETTE STITCH

SCARF

Cast on 45 stitches *loosely* with yarn A. Work in stockinette stitch (knit all right-side rows and purl all wrong-side rows) until the piece measures 85"/216 cm, or approximately 340 rows.

Bind off *very loosely.*

FINISHING

Weave in all loose ends with the tapestry needle.

Fold the Scarf in half lengthwise to find the center line and use two pins to mark the center of the cast-on and bind-off edges. Place pins along the cast-on and bind-off edges 1½"/ 3.8 cm from each side.

Cut three strands of yarn B approximately 100"/254 cm long. Thread the tapestry needle with one strand of yarn. Start at one of the center pins and weave the strand of yarn in and out along this center fold line following the same column of stitches to maintain a straight line. Each woven segment should be about 2"/5 cm, or 8 rows of stitches. Weave the other two strands of yarn B along the two imaginary lines marked by the pins 1½"/3.8 cm from each side edge (see weaving diagram).

With the tapestry needle, loop the ends of each woven length of yarn B around the cast-on and bind-off edges of the scarf and reinsert these ends through the same holes, leaving a 7"/18 cm tail (see photograph).

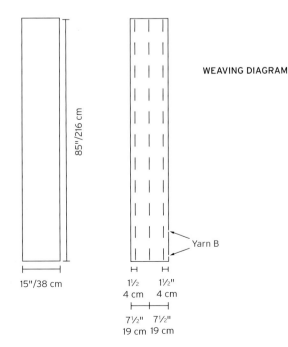

85"/216 cm

15"/38 cm

WEAVING DIAGRAM

Yarn B

1½"   1½"
4 cm   4 cm

7½"   7½"
19 cm   19 cm

soft fringed shawl

YOU WILL LOVE KNITTING THIS TRIANGLE-SHAPED SHAWL IN AN EASY STITCH ON HUGE SIZE 50 NEEDLES. IT ENDS UP VERY LOOSE, OPEN, AND MODERN-LOOKING, BUT THE HAND-TIED FRINGE GIVES IT A CLASSIC LOOK. THE BABY ALPACA YARN IS PERFECT FOR WEEKEND GETAWAYS BECAUSE IT'S SO LIGHT AND VERSATILE. YOU CAN WEAR IT AROUND YOUR NECK AS AN ACCESSORY, YOUR WAIST AS A BEACH COVER-UP, OR YOUR SHOULDERS ON A CHILLY EVENING.

SIZE
ONE SIZE FITS ALL

FINISHED MEASUREMENTS
APPROXIMATELY 64" WIDE X 40" LONG/162.5 CM X 101.5 CM
   (SEE DIAGRAM)

YARN
2 SKEINS SUSS FISHNET (53% ACRYLIC/30% NYLON/17%
   ALPACA; 1½ OUNCES/43 GRAMS; 285 YARDS/261
   METERS), COLOR PUMPKIN

NOTIONS
1 PAIR SIZE 50 (25 MM) NEEDLES
1 LARGE TAPESTRY NEEDLE
POINT PROTECTORS (RECOMMENDED)
1 SIZE G (4 MM) CROCHET HOOK

GAUGE
4 STITCHES AND 4 ROWS = 4"/10 CM IN
   STOCKINETTE STITCH
A NOTE ABOUT GAUGE: BECAUSE OF THE LIGHT AND AIRY
   EFFECT OF KNITTING LACY YARN ON LARGE NEEDLES,
   PRECISE GAUGE IS DIFFICULT TO MEASURE AND, FOR
   THIS PROJECT, NOT REALLY NECESSARY.

SHAWL

Cast on 4 stitches. Work even in stockinette stitch (knit all right-side rows and purl all wrong-side rows) for 1 row. Increase 1 stitch at the beginning of every row 16 times—17 rows, 20 stitches.

Cast on 2 stitches at the beginning of every row 22 times—39 rows, 64 stitches. Work 1 row even—40 rows.

Bind off *loosely*.

FINISHING

Weave in all loose ends with the tapestry needle.

To make the fringe, cut the yarn into 34 strands 11"/28 cm long. With the crochet hook, attach the fringe by folding one strand in half and pulling this folded loop through the edge of the Shawl. Pull the ends through this loop and tighten. Attach approximately 17 fringe tassels on each of the narrow edges of the Shawl, spacing them about 3"/7.5 cm apart. The fringe should have a loose and airy look, but you don't need to be very precise with its placement.

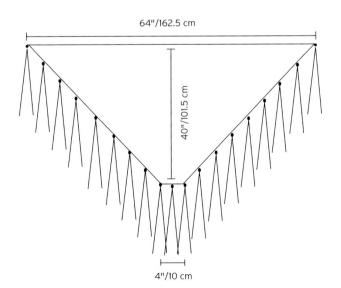

64"/162.5 cm

40"/101.5 cm

4"/10 cm

lined purse
with chain handle

CAN YOU GUESS WHAT DESIGNER I WAS THINKING ABOUT WHEN I CREATED THIS PURSE? WITH A CHAIN HANDLE AND BUCKLES, IT HAS TO BE CHANEL. TWO-TONED FINE YARN CREATES A HOUNDSTOOTH-LIKE PATTERN—VERY CLASSIC. IF YOU PREFER A MORE CASUAL BAG, JUST SUBSTITUTE A WOODEN HANDLE AND BUTTONS INSTEAD OF BUCKLES. A CUTE LITTLE COSMETIC OR COIN PURSE TO TUCK INSIDE KNITS UP IN AN HOUR OR TWO.

FINISHED MEASUREMENTS
EVENING BAG: 11" WIDE X 7" TALL/28 CM X 18 CM
MINI BAG: 6" WIDE X 4½" TALL/15 CM X 11.5 CM

YARNS
A: 4 SKEINS SUSS MATTE (60% WOOL/40% TACTEL
NYLON; 2 OUNCES/57 GRAMS; 81 YARDS/74 METERS),
COLOR BERRY
B: 3 SKEINS SUSS SHINE (100% VISCOSE; 1 OUNCE/28
GRAMS; 136 YARDS/124 METERS), COLOR BLACK CHERRY

NOTIONS
1 PAIR SIZE 10.5 (6.5 MM) NEEDLES
1 LARGE TAPESTRY NEEDLE
1 PIECE ROSE-COLORED VELVET, 10" WIDE X 19" LONG/
25.5 CM X 48 CM
SEWING NEEDLE AND THREAD IN COMPLEMENTARY COLOR
SEWING PINS (OPTIONAL)
2 GOLD BUCKLES, 1½"/3.8 CM WIDE (AVAILABLE AT MOST
CRAFT OR SEWING STORES)
1 GOLD CHAIN APPROXIMATELY ½"/13 MM WIDE AND 22"/
56 CM LONG (AVAILABLE AT MOST HARDWARE STORES)
1 RED ZIPPER 6"/15 CM LONG

GAUGE
17 STITCHES AND 20 ROWS = 4"/10 CM IN DOUBLE SEED
STITCH WITH YARNS A AND B HELD TOGETHER

DOUBLE SEED STITCH PATTERN

Rows 1 and 2: *Knit 1, purl 1*, repeat from * to * until end of row.

Rows 3 and 4: *Purl 1, knit 1*, repeat from * to * until end of row.

Repeat Rows 1–4.

PURSE

Cast on 48 stitches with one strand of yarn A and one strand of yarn B held together.

Work in double seed stitch pattern.

Bind off in pattern until piece measures 20"/51 cm.

STRAPS (Make two)

Cast on 6 stitches.

Work in double seed stitch pattern until piece measures 4"/10 cm.

Bind off in pattern.

FINISHING

Weave in all loose ends with the tapestry needle.

With the tapestry needle and one strand of yarn A and one strand of yarn B held together, attach the evening bag Straps to the right side of the knitted Purse approximately 2"/5 cm from the corners (see diagram for placement). Use tiny stitches that do not show on the right side. Attach the decorative buckles between the Straps and the right side of the front flap of the Purse so the bottom edge of each buckle is even with the cast-on edge.

Place the velvet lining on top of the wrong side of the knitted piece approximately ½"/13 mm from the edges of the knitted piece. With the sewing needle and thread, whipstitch the velvet lining to the edges of the knitted piece. You may find it helpful to pin the lining to the Purse first.

Fold the Purse in thirds widthwise with the wrong side (lining) facing out (see diagram for fold measurements). With the tapestry needle and one strand of yarn A and one strand of yarn B held together, sew together the sides of the purse using backstitch. Turn the bag right-side out.

With the tapestry needle and one strand of yarn A and one strand of yarn B held together, attach the ends of the chain securely to the bag.

MINI PURSE

Cast on 26 stitches.

Work in double seed stitch pattern until the piece measures 9"/23 cm.

Bind off in pattern.

FINISHING

Fold knitted piece in half widthwise with the right sides facing each other (see diagram). With the tapestry needle and one strand of yarn A and one strand of yarn B held together, sew together the side seams using backstitch. Turn the bag right-side out.

With the sewing needle and thread, whipstitch the cast-on and bind-off edges very close to the zipper.

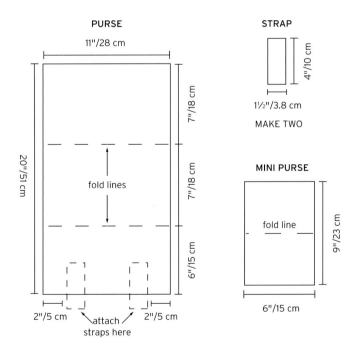

PURSE

11"/28 cm

7"/18 cm

20"/51 cm

fold lines

7"/18 cm

6"/15 cm

2"/5 cm   2"/5 cm

attach straps here

STRAP

4"/10 cm

1½"/3.8 cm

MAKE TWO

MINI PURSE

fold line

9"/23 cm

6"/15 cm

swedish hat with fair isle

MY MOM MADE ME A VERSION OF THIS HAT IN A NORDIC PATTERN WHEN I WAS NINE YEARS OLD. IT'S A CLASSIC, UNI-SEX DESIGN, AND THE EASY COLOR WORK IS MAINLY STRIPES. IT COVERS YOUR EARS TO KEEP YOU WARM FOR FUN IN THE SNOW, AND IT'S ALSO COOL TO WEAR IN THE CITY.

SIZE
ADULT, ONE SIZE FITS ALL

FINISHED MEASUREMENTS
18" WIDE X 9" LONG/46 CM X 23 CM (WITHOUT EAR FLAPS)

YARN
A: 1 SKEIN SUSS ULL (100% WOOL; 2 OUNCES/57 GRAMS; 215 YARDS/197 METERS), COLOR STONE
B: 1 SKEIN SUSS ULL (100% WOOL; 2 OUNCES/57 GRAMS; 215 YARDS/197 METERS), COLOR ARAN
C: 1 SKEIN SUSS ULL (100% WOOL; 2 OUNCES/57 GRAMS; 215 YARDS/197 METERS), COLOR STORM

NOTIONS
1 PAIR SIZE 10 (6 MM) NEEDLES
2 YARN BOBBINS FOR FAIR ISLE TECHNIQUE (OPTIONAL)
1 TAPESTRY NEEDLE
1 SIZE G (4 MM) CROCHET HOOK
POM-POM MAKER (OPTIONAL)

GAUGE
16 STITCHES AND 20 ROWS = 4"/10 CM IN STOCKINETTE STITCH WITH TWO STRANDS OF YARN HELD TOGETHER
NOTE: SINCE THIS PROJECT IS WORKED WITH TWO STRANDS OF YARN HELD TOGETHER, THE FIRST THING YOU SHOULD DO IS DIVIDE EACH SKEIN INTO TWO BALLS OF EQUAL SIZE.

EAR FLAPS

Cast on 4 stitches with two strands of yarn A held together. Work in stockinette stitch (knit all right-side rows and purl all wrong-side rows). Work 1 row even.

Increase 1 stitch at the beginning and end of every wrong-side row 6 times—16 stitches total. Increase 1 stitch at the beginning and end of every other wrong-side row 1 time—18 stitches total. Work even until ear flap measures 4"/10 cm from the cast-on edge, or approximately 20 rows, ending with a wrong-side row.

Cut yarn, leaving a 30"/76 cm tail. Leave this ear flap on the left-hand needle and work a second ear flap in the same way as the first. You should have two ear flaps (with right-sides facing you) on the left-hand needle.

On the rightmost ear flap (the one attached to the working yarn), cast on 10 stitches, knit across those 10 stitches and the 18 stitches of the ear flap—28 stitches total.

To cast on new stitches, insert the right-hand needle into the space between the first 2 stitches on the left-hand needle. Pull the yarn through, making a loop, and place that loop back on the left-hand needle. Repeat until you have cast on the desired number of stitches.

With the 30"/76 cm tail, cast on 16 stitches at the beginning of the other ear flap.

HAT

With the working yarn (attached to ear flap on right needle), join and knit across these 16 stitches and the 18 stitches of the second ear flap—62 stitches total on needle. Turn and cast on 10 stitches at beginning of next row—72 stitches total. Purl all 72 stitches in row.

Work even for 8 rows—10 rows total (not including ear flaps).

Change to yarn B and work even for 2 rows—12 rows total.

Note: Continue working with two strands of yarn throughout.

Change to yarn A and work even for 2 rows—14 rows total.

Change to yarn B and work even for 2 rows—16 rows total.

Change to yarn A and work even for 4 rows—20 rows total.

Change to yarn B and begin 7-row Fair Isle pattern (see chart). (You may find it helpful to work yarns B and C from yarn bobbins.) Repeat 8-stitch sequence on chart until end of row—27 rows total.

Change to yarn A and work even for 4 rows—31 rows total.

Change to yarn B and work even for 2 rows—33 rows total.

Change to yarn A and work even for 2 rows—35 rows total.

Change to yarn B and work even for 2 rows—37 rows total.

Change to yarn A and work even for 8 rows—45 rows total.

Do not bind off. Instead, cut yarn about 36"/91.5 cm from knitting needle and thread the end through the tapestry needle. Insert the tapestry needle into the first stitch knitwise and thread it through all the stitches on the knitting needle. Remove the knitting needle slowly as you thread through each of the stitches. Pull the yarn taut, forming a tight circle. Tie the yarn off but *do not cut the tail.*

With this tail, sew together the back seam of the hat using backstitch.

FINISHING

Weave in all loose ends with the tapestry needle.

With the crochet hook and two strands of yarn A, join and work a single crochet stitch along the entire bottom hem of the hat, including the Ear Flaps.

TIES

Cut yarn A into 24 strands, each approximately 30"/76 cm long. Take 12 strands of yarn and fold them in half, forming a loop. With the crochet hook, draw that loop through the bottom of one of the Ear Flaps (see diagram) from the back to the front. Pull the strands of yarn through that loop and tighten.

Divide into 3 groups of 8 strands and braid the tie until approximately 4"/10 cm remains and tie a tight knot.

Repeat for the second Ear Flap.

Make a pom-pom using yarn C. You can use a pom-pom maker or do it yourself by wrapping the yarn around a stiff piece of cardboard (or something similar) about 4"/10 cm wide. Wrap the yarn around the cardboard until the pom-pom is the desired thickness. Cut the yarn about 20"/51 cm from the cardboard. Thread the end of the yarn through the tapestry needle and wrap it three times around the center of the pom-pom loops, pulling it tight. Pull the pom-pom off the piece of cardboard. Make a strong, tight knot in the yarn wrapped around the center of the pom-pom. Cut the ends of the pom-pom loops and trim to form a ball.

Attach pom-pom to the top center of the hat with the tapestry needle and yarn C.

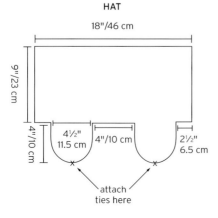

HAT

18"/46 cm

9"/23 cm

4"/10 cm

4½"
11.5 cm

4"/10 cm

2½"
6.5 cm

attach ties here

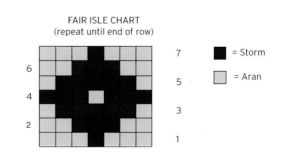

FAIR ISLE CHART
(repeat until end of row)

1 2 3 4 5 6 7

■ = Storm

☐ = Aran

long sampler scarf

WHEN IT COMES TO SCARVES, THE POSSIBILITIES ARE ENDLESS. THE COCO BURST YARN AND RUFFLED EDGES USED FOR THIS DESIGN ARE SO LUXURIOUS THAT THE SCARF ALMOST RESEMBLES A CHOCOLATY LAYERED DESSERT! ALTERNATING SECTIONS OF THICK AND THIN TEXTURE CREATES ULTIMATE SOFTNESS—AND KNITTING THEM WILL KEEP YOU ENTERTAINED.

FINISHED MEASUREMENTS
8" WIDE X 70" LONG/20.5 CM X 178 CM

YARNS
A: 4 SKEINS SUSS LUX (40% COTTON; 40% POLYAMIDE/
   20% RAYON; 2 OUNCES/57 GRAMS; 56 YARDS/51
   METERS), COLOR GRAY
B: 2 SKEINS SUSS COTTON (100% COTTON; 2.5 OUNCES/
   71 GRAMS; 118 YARDS/108 METERS), COLOR CHOCOLATE
C: 2 SKEINS SUSS FANTASY (50% COTTON/15% MOHAIR/
   10% VISCOSE/10% NYLON/10% POLYESTER/5% WOOL;
   4 OUNCES/114 GRAMS; 50 YARDS/46 METERS), COLOR
   COCO BURST

NOTIONS
1 PAIR SIZE 17 (12.75 MM) NEEDLES
1 LARGE TAPESTRY NEEDLE

GAUGE
10 STITCHES AND 12 ROWS = 4"/10 CM IN STOCKINETTE
   STITCH WITH YARN A
10 STITCHES AND 16 ROWS = 4"/10 CM IN GARTER STITCH
   AND TWO STRANDS OF YARN B
10 STITCHES AND 12 ROWS = 4"/10 CM IN MOSS STITCH
   WITH YARN C
10 STITCHES AND 12 ROWS = 4"/10 CM IN DIAGONAL RIB
   STITCH AND TWO STRANDS OF YARN A

MOSS STITCH PATTERN

Rows 1 and 2: *Knit 1, purl 1*, repeat from * to * until end of row.

Rows 3 and 4: *Purl 1, knit 1*, repeat from * to * until end of row.

Repeat Rows 1–4.

DIAGONAL RIB STITCH PATTERN

Row 1: *Knit 3, purl 3*, repeat across row.

Row 2: Purl 1, *knit 3, purl 3*, repeat from * to * until 2 stitches remain, purl 2.

Row 3: Knit 1, *purl 3, knit 3*, repeat from * to * until 2 stitches remain, knit 2.

Row 4: Purl 3, *knit 3, purl 3*, repeat from * to * until 3 stitches remain, knit 3.

Row 5: Purl 2, *knit 3, purl 3*, repeat from * to * until 1 stitch remains, purl 1.

Row 6: Knit 2, *purl 3, knit 3*, repeat from * to * until 1 stitch remains, knit 1.

Repeat Rows 1–6.

SCARF

Cast on 54 stitches with one strand of yarn A. Work in stockinette stitch (knit all right-side rows and purl all wrong-side rows) for 3"/7.5 cm, ending with a wrong-side row.

Switch to two strands of yarn B held together. Knit 3 stitches together across entire row—18 stitches total. Work in garter stitch (knit all rows) for 3"/7.5 cm, 6"/15 cm from the cast-on edge, ending with a wrong-side row.

Switch to yarn C and work in moss stitch for 5"/12.5 cm, 11"/28 cm from the cast-on edge, ending with either Row 2 or Row 4.

Switch to two strands of yarn B held together. Work in garter stitch for 3"/7.5 cm, 14"/35.5 cm from the cast-on edge, ending with a wrong-side row.

Switch to two strands of yarn A held together. Work in diagonal rib stitch for 5"/12.5 cm, 19"/48 cm from the cast-on edge, ending with a wrong-side row.

Switch to two strands of yarn B held together. Work in garter stitch for 3"/7.5 cm, 22"/56 cm from the cast-on edge, ending with a wrong-side row.

Switch to yarn C and work in moss stitch for 5"/12.5 cm, 27"/68.5 cm from the cast-on edge, ending with a wrong-side row.

Switch to two strands of yarn B held together. Work in garter stitch for 3"/7.5 cm, 30"/76 cm from the cast-on edge, ending with a wrong-side row.

Switch to two strands of yarn A held together. Work in diagonal rib stitch for 10"/25.5 cm, 40"/101.5 cm from the cast-on edge, ending with a wrong-side row.

Switch to two strands of yarn B held together. Work in garter stitch for 3"/7.5 cm, 43"/109 cm from the cast-on edge, ending with a wrong-side row.

Switch to yarn C and work in moss stitch for 5"/12.5 cm, 48"/122 cm from the cast-on edge, ending with a wrong-side row.

Switch to two strands of yarn B held together. Work in garter stitch for 3"/7.5 cm, 51"/129.5 cm from the cast-on edge, ending with a wrong-side row.

Switch to two strands of yarn A held together. Work in diagonal rib stitch for 5"/12.5 cm, 56"/142 cm from the cast-on edge, ending with a wrong-side row.

Switch to two strands of yarn B held together. Work in garter stitch for 3"/7.5 cm, 59"/150 cm from the cast-on edge, ending with a wrong-side row.

Switch to yarn C and work in moss stitch for 5"/12.5 cm, 64"/162.5 cm from the cast-on edge, ending with a wrong-side row.

Switch to two strands of yarn B held together. Work in garter stitch for 3"/7.5 cm, 67"/170 cm from the cast-on edge, ending with a wrong-side row.

Switch to one strand of yarn A. Increase 2 stitches in every stitch as follows: Knit stitch through the front loop, but *do not* slip stitch from left-hand needle. Knit stitch through back loop, but *do not* slip stitch from left-hand needle. Knit stitch through front loop again and slip stitch from left needle—54 stitches total.

Work in stockinette stitch for 3"/7.5 cm, 70"/178 cm from the cast-on edge, ending with a wrong-side row.

Bind off loosely.

FINISHING Weave in all loose ends with the tapestry needle.

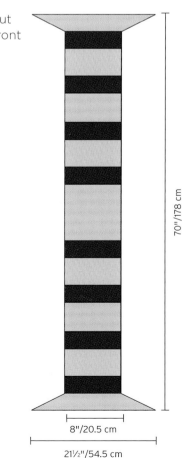

= Gray

= Chocolate

= Coco Burst

70"/178 cm

8"/20.5 cm

21½"/54.5 cm

half-moon bag with flowers

THIS PROJECT IS SO FUN! THE COMBINATION OF THE HAND-STITCHED FLOWERS AND THE RED AND CAMEL VARIEGATED YARN GIVE THIS PURSE A PAINTING-LIKE QUALITY. IF YOU PREFER, REPLACE THE FLOWER WITH A DIFFERENT SHAPE: A BIRD, A LEAF, OR ANYTHING WITH A UNIQUE STITCH WILL WORK. HANDLES WITH BEADED WOOD STRINGS WRAPPED AROUND THE EDGES ADD A RUSTIC TOUCH.

FINISHED MEASUREMENTS
APPROXIMATELY 18" WIDE X 10" TALL/46 CM X 25.5 CM

YARNS
A: 3 SKEINS SUSS COOLAID (85% ACRYLIC/15% WOOL;
2 OUNCES/57 GRAMS; 90 YARDS/82 METERS), COLOR
CRANBERRY
B: 3 SKEINS SUSS COOLAID (85% ACRYLIC/15% WOOL;
2 OUNCES/57 GRAMS; 90 YARDS/82 METERS),
COLOR HONEY

NOTIONS
1 PAIR SIZE 11 (8 MM) NEEDLES
1 LARGE TAPESTRY NEEDLE
SEWING NEEDLE AND TAN-COLORED THREAD
SEWING PINS (OPTIONAL)
½ YARD/.5 METER CORAL-COLORED LINEN FABRIC
2 CANVAS BEADED HORSESHOE-SHAPED HANDLES, 7½"/19
CM WIDE (AVAILABLE AT WWW.SUSSDESIGN.COM)
2 CROCHETED BROWN FELT FLOWERS (AVAILABLE AT
WWW.SUSSDESIGN.COM)

GAUGE
12 STITCHES AND 14 ROWS = 4"/10 CM IN STOCKINETTE
STITCH WITH TWO STRANDS HELD TOGETHER

BAG

Cast on 54 stitches with one strand of yarn A and one strand of yarn B held together.

Work in stockinette stitch (knit all right-side rows and purl all wrong-side rows). Decrease 1 stitch at the beginning and end of every 4 rows 5 times—44 stitches, 20 rows. Decrease 1 stitch at the beginning and end of every 3 rows 5 times—34 stitches, 35 rows.

Work 1 row even—36 rows.

Increase 1 stitch at the beginning and end of the next row and every 3 rows thereafter 4 times—44 stitches, 49 rows. Work even for 2 rows—51 rows. Increase 1 stitch at the beginning and end of the next row and every 4 rows thereafter 4 times—54 stitches, 68 rows. Work even for 3 rows—71 rows total.

Bind off.

FINISHING

Weave in all loose ends with the tapestry needle.

Fold the Bag in half widthwise with the purl sides facing each other. With the tapestry needle and yarn A, backstitch the side seams together securely with a small seam allowance. Turn the Bag so that the purl side is on the outside of the Bag.

Center the flowers on each side of the Bag and pin in place. With the sewing needle and thread, whipstitch the two crocheted flowers securely to the outside of the bag. Make small tacking stitches to ensure that each of the petals lies flat on the Bag. This will also keep the petals from getting caught on things or getting bent out of shape.

LINING

Using the shape of the Bag to guide you, cut the fabric into two pieces slightly smaller than the Bag itself. With the *right sides facing each other,* pin the two pieces of fabric to each other. With the sewing needle and thread, sew the two pieces together, leaving the top edge unseamed. Place this lining "bag" inside the knitted Bag, fold over the top edge approximately ½"/13 mm, and pin in place. With the sewing needle and thread, whipstitch the lining securely to the inside of the knitted Bag.

With the tapestry needle and yarn B, attach the handles securely to the center of the top edge of the Bag.

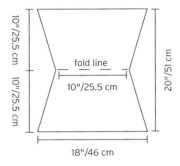

acknowledgments

First, thank you, readers, for your support of my books and my designs.

The wonderful friends in my life who happily participated as models in my book are why it has such a warm feeling.

Thanks to:

Taiye Adeagbo

Hanna Cousins

Yoshie Eenigenberg

Ariana Gabisan

Robin Glaser

Fanahi Williams.

And thanks to the following models for your great work:

Kate Amundsen

Hilary Greenleaf.

Very special thanks to:

Yoshie Eenigenburg for helping me pull this book together, both with design, styling, and all the other ways you help me every day.

Kate Lonsdale, who has gotten very familiar with my work as she helps with pattern making. You do an incredible job!

To all of you at the Suss Design Store and Studio for being by my side through my adventures. Thanks for your continuing good work. I love you always.

Jennifer Gross and Evolutionary Media. Thanks for being such a great friend.

Photographer Suzuki K and her partner, Gene Shibuya. Thanks for making this beautiful book come to life with your wonderful eye.

The Hiroshi Watanabe Studio.

International Silks and Woolens, my neighbors on Beverly Boulevard. Your staff always offers me extraspecial service.

Lesly Polig for the fun hairstyles.

Karen Greenwald for technical editing.

Robin Dellabough of Lark Productions for yet another venture together. It's been a great ride. Thanks for always keeping me on track, Robin!

Everyone at Potter Craft. Each book is better than the last.

And to Brian and my two wonderful girls, Hanna and Viveka. Thanks for being in my life and giving me positive energy and love so I can continue making more books. You mean everything to me.

resources

Yarn

Suss yarn is available at Suss Design, 7350 Beverly Boulevard, Los Angeles, California 90036 (telephone: 323-954-9637). The store stocks Suss brand yarns and yarns from all the best manufacturers. Shoppers can also find needles, patterns, and a complete collection of notions (buttons, beads, and crochet and leather decorations) needed for projects in Suss's books.

Knitters around the country can purchase Suss yarns at the Suss Design website, www.sussdesign.com.

Stores that carry Suss Yarn:

Alabama
In the Making
3118 Heights Village
Birmingham, AL 35243
205-298-1309

Taming of the Ewe
255 Co. Rd. 263
Piedmont, AL 36265
678-294-5065

Alaska
Yarn Branch of the
Quilt Tree
341 E. Benson #5
Anchorage, AK 99503
907-561-4115

California
Article Pract
5010 Telegraph Ave.
Oakland, CA 94609
510-595-7875

Devrie Christina's Knittery
1202 Grant Ave., Ste. A1
Novato, CA 94945
415-236-1536

Fabric Town USA
2686 E. Main St.
Ventura, CA 93003
805-643-3434

Harriets Yarns
77-780 Country
Club Dr., Ste. A
Palm Desert, CA 92211
760-772-3333

Knitting by the Beach
616 Stevens Avenue, Ste. B
Solana Beach, CA 92075
858-509-9276

A Mano Yarn Center
12808 Venice Blvd.
Los Angeles, CA 90066
310-397-7170

Three Dog Knit
475 N. Lake Blvd., Ste. 103
Tahoe City, CA 96145
530-583-0001

Yarn Company of
Palm Desert
73445 El Paseo, Ste. 12E
Palm Desert, CA 92260
760-341-7734

Yarning for You
1001 W. San Marcos
Blvd. #180
San Marcos, CA 92078
760-744-5648

Yarn Paper Scissors
1410 B Burlingame Ave.
Burlingame, CA 94010
650-348-1425

Connecticut
Knitting Central
582 Post Rd. East
Westport, CT 06880
203-454-4300

Sit 'N' Knit
33 LaSalle Rd.
West Hartford, CT 06107
860-232-9276

Georgia
Knitch
1025 St. Charles Ave. NE
Atlanta, GA 30306
404-745-9276

Idaho
Isabel's Needlepoint
4th St.
Ketchum, ID 83340
888-267-0114

Illinois
Chix with Stix
7316 W. Madison St.
Forest Park, IL 60130
708-366-6300

Loopy Yarns
719 S. State St.
Chicago, IL 60605
312-583-9276

My Sister's Knits
9907 S. Walden Parkway
Chicago, IL 60643
773-238-4555

Nina
1655 W. Division St.
Chicago, IL 60622
773-486-8996

Michigan
Hampton Mills
576 N. Old Woodward Ave.
Birmingham, MI 48009
248-593-8559

Minnesota
Digs
310 Division St. South
Northfield, MN 55057
507-664-9140

New York
The Knitting Place
191 Main St.
Port Washington, NY 11050
516-944-9276

New York Knits
1286 Blossom Dr.
Victor, NY 14564
585-924-1950

Wild Wools
732 South Ave.
Rochester, NY 14620
585-271-0960

A Yarn For All Seasons
8240 Cazenovia Rd.,
Ste. 100
Manlius, NY 13104
315-692-4580

Ohio
The Knitting Garden
25887 Detroit Rd.
Westlake, OH 44145
440-250-5648

Oklahoma
Loops
2042 Utica Sq. West
Tulsa, OK 74114
918-742-9276

Pennsylvania
Forever Yarn
15 W. Oakland Ave.
Doylestown, PA 18901
215-348-5648

Knit One 2721
2721 Murray Ave.
Pittsburgh, PA 15217
412-421-6666

Knitting to Know Ewe
2324 Second St. Pike, #370
Penns Park, PA 18943
215-598-9276

Loop
1914 South St.
Philadelphia, PA 19146
215-893-9939

South Dakota
Yarn Knit
401 E. 8th Street
Sioux Falls, SD 57103
605-330-9276

Washington, DC
Stitch DC
5520 Connecticut
Ave., NW
Washington, DC 20015
202-237-8306

Canada
Cricket Cove Handknits
836 Main St.
Blacks Harbor, NB
Canada E5H1E6
506-456-3897

Room 6
4389 Gallant Ave.
North Vancouver, BC
Canada V7G1L1
604-628-8484

yarn substitution guide

The following guide, organized by yarn weight, lists all the Suss yarns used in this book and offers suggestions for substitution. In some cases, you will need to combine yarns to create an effect similar to that of a Suss yarn. With those substitutions, please pay extra attention to your gauge. As always, if you're not sure whether a particular yarn can be used as a substitute, try knitting a swatch first to determine if the gauge matches. The fabric should also be similar in drape, texture, and appearance. The amount of yarn per skein varies, so be sure you base your substitution on the total yardage rather than the number of skeins.

2 **Fine (Sport, Baby)**
Suss Bamboo: Bamboo Soft by Rowan; Hempathy by Elsebeth Lavold; Linie 163 Bingo by Online; Linie 28 Borneo by Online; 4-Ply Cotton by Rowan; or any fingering-weight mercerized cotton or 100% rayon.
Suss Old Fashioned: Silky Wool by Elsebeth Lavold; 4-Ply Scottish Tweed by Rowan (may need to be doubled); or any tweedy wool yarn of comparable weight.
Suss Shine: Rayon by Swallow Hill; Glowette by Erdal; or any shiny, viscose-blend carry-along yarn of comparable weight and texture.

3 **Light (DK, Light Worsted)**
Suss Angora: Misti Alpaca Lace by Misti Alpaca Yarns; Cashsoft 4-Ply by Rowan; Fingering-Weight Alpaca by Frog Tree Yarns; or any angora or cashmere blend of comparable weight.
Suss Fishnet: Kidsilk Haze by Rowan; Kid Merino by Crystal Palace; Lace Mohair by Karabella; or Kid Mohair by Louet (all may need to be doubled).
Suss Nubby: Cotton Flamme by Crystal Palace or Cotton Flake by Ironstone.
Suss Perle Cotton: Six Two or Baby Georgia by Crystal Palace; Dream by Tahki Yarns; Pastimes Too by Conjoined Creations; or Perle Cotton #5 by DMC (for embroidery on Embroidered Dress only).
Suss Tonal: Suss Tonal consists of a double strand of Suss Fishnet in two complementary colors. See substitutes for Suss Fishnet (above).
Suss Ull: Cascade 220 by Cascade Yarns; Wollywasch by GGH; Superwash by Lamb's Pride; Merino DK by Debbie Bliss; or O-Wool Classic by Vermont Organic Fiber.
Suss Ultrasoft: Suss Ultrasoft is a shiny, nubby, laceweight rayon carry-along yarn combined with a light kid mohair yarn similar to Suss Fishnet. Skinny Majestic by Grand River is one possible substitute.

4 **Medium (Worsted, Afghan, Aran)**
Suss Alpaca: Alpaca Silk by Blue Sky Alpacas; Baby Suri Silk by Misti Alpaca Yarns; Light-Weight Cashmere by Karabella; or Alpaca Sport by Frog Tree Yarns.
Suss Alpaca Tweed: Inca Marl by Classic Elite; Aran Marl by Crystal Palace; or Alpaca Seta by Skacel.
Suss Bomull: Cotton DK by Debbie Bliss; Denim by Rowan; or All Season Cotton by Rowan.
Suss Cotton: Dyed or Organic Cotton by Blue Sky Alpacas; Cotton Stria by Manos del Uruguay; or 1824 Cotton by Mission Falls.

Suss Crunch: Suss Crunch consists of a double-stranded combination of a light mohair-merino laceweight yarn similar to Suss Fishnet combined with a DK-weight nonmercerized cotton similar to Suss Nubby. See Suss Fishnet and Suss Nubby (both on previous page) for substitutions.

Suss Love: Baby Cashmerino or Cashmerino Aran by Debbie Bliss (pay close attention to gauge); Cashsoft DK by Rowan; or Smooth DK by King Cole.

Suss Matte: Create an effect similar to Suss Matte by combining a DK-weight wool similar to Suss Ull (see substitutions on previous page) with a silky ribbon yarn such as Sevilla by Katia, Silk Ribbon by Artyarns, Mikado Ribbon Solid by Crystal Palace, or Bonsai by Berroco.

Suss Mohair: La Gran Mohair by Classic Elite; Ingenua by Katia; or Fumo by Lana Grossa.

Suss Royal: Ibis by Classic Elite (may need double to obtain gauge); Dune by Trendsetter; or Kid Slique by Prism.

Suss Rustic: Dreamy by Kollage Yarns. You can also mimic Suss Rustic by combining a DK-weight wool such as Suss Ull (see substitutions on previous page) with a soft, nylon, novelty, carry-along puff yarn similar to Tootsie by Trendsetter.

Suss Snuggle: Samoa or Bali by GGH (depending on gauge obtained); Wool Cotton by Rowan; or Diana by Katia.

5 Bulky (Chunky, Craft, Rug)

Suss Butterfly: Passion by Kollage Yarns. You can also mimic Suss Butterfly by combining Voila by Trendsetter with Papi or Joy by Trendsetter.

Suss Coolaid: Big Wool by Rowan; Iceland by Crystal Palace; or Lamb's Pride Bulky by Brown Sheep.

Suss Fuzzy: Amelie by GGH or Pep by Lana Grossa. You can also mimic the effect of Suss Fuzzy by combining cotton similar to Suss Bomull (see substitutions on previous page) with a soft novelty yarn similar to Voila by Trendsetter or Whisper by Crystal Palace.

Suss Lux: Mimic the effect of Suss Lux by combining bulky cotton similar to Suss Natural Soft (see subsitutions below) with a soft novelty yarn similar to Voila by Trendsetter.

Suss Natural Soft: Drops Ice by Garnstudio; Leisure by Cascade; or Aspen by Ornaghi Filati.

6 Super Bulky (Bulky, Roving)

Suss Fantasy: Captive Lash or Splendor by Kollage Yarns (may need to be doubled); Light Stuff, Cool Stuff, or Neat Stuff by Prism.

yarn weight symbol & category name	2 FINE	3 LIGHT	4 MEDIUM	5 BULKY	6 SUPER BULKY
other names of yarns	sport, baby	DK, light worsted four-ply, jumper	worsted, afghan, aran	chunky, craft, rug	bulky, roving
knit gauge range in stockinette stitch to 4 inches (10cm)	23–26 stitches	21–24 stitches	16–20 stitches	12–15 stitches	6–11 stitches
recomended needle size range	U.S. 3–5 (3.25–3.75mm)	U.S. 5–7 (3.25–4.5mm)	U.S. 7–9 (4.5–5.5mm)	U.S. 9–11 (5.5–8mm)	U.S. 3–5 (8mm and larger)

index

suss design essentials